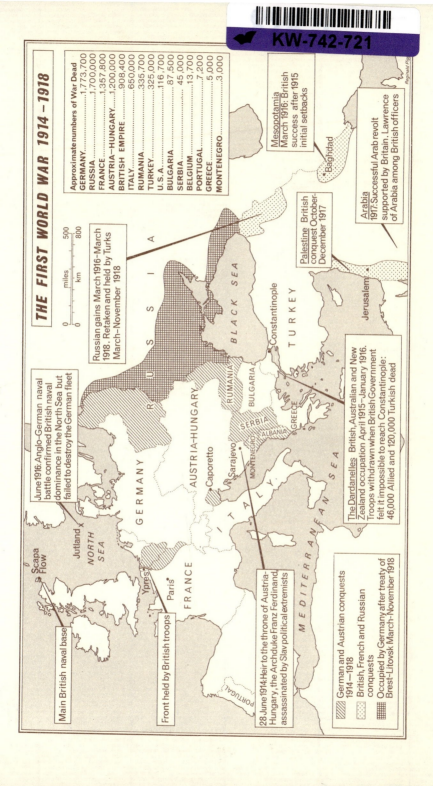

THE FIRST WORLD WAR 1914 – 1918

Reginald Piggott

Approximate numbers of War Dead

GERMANY	1,773,700
RUSSIA	1,700,000
FRANCE	1,357,800
AUSTRIA–HUNGARY	1,200,000
BRITISH EMPIRE	908,400
ITALY	650,000
RUMANIA	335,700
TURKEY	325,000
U.S.A.	116,700
BULGARIA	87,500
SERBIA	45,000
BELGIUM	13,700
PORTUGAL	7,200
GREECE	5,000
MONTENEGRO	3,000

Mesopotamia March 1916: British success after 1915 initial setbacks

Arabia 1917: Successful Arab revolt supported by Britain. Lawrence of Arabia among British officers

Russian gains March 1916–March 1918. Retaken and held by Turks March–November 1918

Palestine British conquest October–December 1917

June 1916: Anglo-German naval battle confirmed British naval dominance in the North Sea but failed to destroy the German fleet

The Dardanelles British, Australian and New Zealand occupation April 1915–January 1916. Troops withdrawn when British Government felt it impossible to reach Constantinople: 46,000 Allied and 120,000 Turkish dead

Main British naval base

Front held by British troops

28 June 1914: Heir to the throne of Austria-Hungary, the Archduke Franz Ferdinand, assassinated by Slav political extremists

miles 500
km 800

Baghdad

Jerusalem

Constantinople

Scapa Flow
Jutland
NORTH SEA
Ypres
Paris
FRANCE
GERMANY
RUSSIA
AUSTRIA–HUNGARY
Caporetto
Sarajevo
ITALY
SERBIA
MONTENEGRO
ALBANIA
RUMANIA
BULGARIA
GREECE
BLACK SEA
TURKEY
MEDITERRANEAN SEA
PORTUGAL

German and Austrian conquests 1914–1918

British, French and Russian conquests

Occupied by Germany after treaty of Brest–Litovsk March–November 1918

WHAT GREATER GLORY?

A Scrapbook of the First World War

The Menin Road by Paul Nash

WHAT GREATER GLORY?

A Scrapbook of the First World War

B. W. Caws, M.A.
Principal Lecturer
The College of Education
Bognor Regis, Sussex

R. F. Watts, M.A.
Head of the English Department
Teignmouth Grammar School
Teignmouth, Devon

Blackie

Blackie & Son Limited
Bishopbriggs, Glasgow G64 2NZ
5 Fitzhardinge Street, London W1H 0DL

© B. W. Caws and R. F. Watts 1974
First published 1974

Educational Edition ISBN 0 216 89778 5
General Edition ISBN 0 216 89727 0

Printed in Great Britain
by Robert MacLehose and Company Limited, Glasgow

FOREWORD

Literature does not exist in a vacuum, and it is our belief that twentieth-century poetry and prose is illuminated by seeing it in relation to contemporary art, photography, song and propaganda. This is certainly true of such a turbulent period as The First World War. In this book we have attempted to recapture the atmosphere of the period and the emotions of the people concerned. We have focussed the picture on the Western Front because out of that uniquely horrific combination of mass armies, machinery and mud, there grew a uniquely moving and enduring literature. This is not a history book, nor does it claim to be exhaustive in the coverage of the literature. What it does claim to do is to tell a powerful story and to tell it primarily through the talents of the men who were eye-witnesses—men who were there.

What we hope is that those who read this book will be inspired to read further and to find out more about a war that brought out some of the best as well as some of the worst in human nature. We hope that the book will be a memorable and moving experience for those who read it and that it will afford a glimpse into the life and times of the people involved.

B. W. Caws
R. F. Watts

ACKNOWLEDGMENTS

For permission to reproduce copyright material in this anthology, the compilers and publishers would like to thank the following: The Imperial War Museum for the frontispiece and the photographs on pages 2, 10, 29, 34, 39, 50, 76 and 83; Cassell & Co. Ltd. for the extracts from *Life for Life's Sake* by Richard Aldington and *Tell England* by Ernest Raymond; Chappell & Co. Ltd. for the chorus from "Your King and Country Want You" by Paul Rubens; Constable & Co. Ltd. for "Fall In" from *Fighting Lines* by Harold Begbie; George Allen & Unwin Ltd. for the extract from Volume II of Bertrand Russell's *Autobiography*; Ullstein Bilderdienst for the photograph on page 12; Robert Graves for the extract from *Goodbye to All That* and "The Morning Before the Battle" and "Sergeant-Major Money" from *The Collected Poems of Robert Graves*; Francis Day & Hunter Ltd. for the chorus from "Goodbye-ee!" by R. P. Weston and Bert Lee and for the verse from "I Know Where to Find 'Em" by L. Barrett; The Estate of H. G. Wells for the extract from *Mr. Britling Sees It Through* by H. G. Wells; Leo Cooper Ltd. for the extract from *The First Hundred Thousand* by Ian Hay; Faber & Faber Ltd. for the extract from *In Parenthesis* by David Jones, "The Happy Warrior" by Herbert Read from *Collected Poems* and the extract from *Outline* by Paul Nash; Robbins Music Corporation for the verses from "I Want to Go Home" by Lt. Gitz Rice and "Over There" by George M. Cohan; Hutchinson Publishing Group Ltd. for the extracts from *The Home Front* by Sylvia Pankhurst and *My War Memories, 1914–18* by General Ludendorff; London Express News & Feature Services for the extract from the *Daily Express* of May 8th, 1915; Milton Waldman and Chatto & Windus Ltd. for "Battery Moving Up to a New Position from Rest Camp: Dawn" from *Ardours and Endurances* by Robert Nichols; The *Tatler & Bystander* for the cartoons by Bruce Bairnsfather on pages 33 and 45; G. T. Sassoon for "The General", "Does It Matter?" and "Memorial Tablet" by Siegfried Sassoon; A. D. Peters & Co. for the extract from *Undertones of War* by Edmund Blunden and "From Albert to Bapaume" by Alec Waugh; Macdonald & Jane's for the extract from *How Dear Is Life* by Henry Williamson; Peter Davies Ltd. for the extracts from *Sagittarius Rising* by Cecil Lewis and *Her Privates We* by Frederic Manning; Mrs. Joan Bruce for the extract from *War Letters to a Wife* by Lt.-Col. Rowland Feilding; Laurence Pollinger and the Estate of the late Mrs. Frieda Lawrence for the extract from D. H. Lawrence's letter to Catherine Carswell from *The Collected Letters of D. H. Lawrence* published by William Heinemann Ltd.; The Bodley Head for the extract from *How We Lived Then* by Mrs. C. S. Peel; Gerald Duckworth & Co. Ltd. for "Judas and the Profiteer" by Osbert Sitwell from *Selected Poems*; Ascherberg, Hopwood and Crew Ltd. for the verse from "I Wore a Tunic" by Jack Mahoney and Percy Wenrich; David Higham Associates Ltd. for the extract from *All Quiet on the Western Front* by Erich Maria Remarque published by Putnam & Co. Ltd.; Granada Publishing Ltd. for the extract from *Disenchantment* by C. E. Montague; J. M. Dent & Sons Ltd. for the extract from *Under Fire* by Henri Barbusse from Everyman's Library Series; M. Gibson and Macmillan, London and Basingstoke, for "Lament" by Wilfrid Wilson Gibson from *Collected Poems*; Martin Gilbert and Weidenfeld & Nicolson Ltd. for permission to redraw the map from page 100 of *A British History Atlas*.

Every effort has been made to trace owners of copyright material but in some cases this has been impossible. The publishers would, however, be glad to hear from any copyright owners not included.

CONTENTS

POSTSCRIPT

PROLOGUE

It is only after a war that the experience of the individual survivor seems to have either interest or value. During a war civilians can think only in terms of "our side" and "their side". All they ask of their men is that they shall win. The individual suffering and cost are veiled behind military phrases, which cushion the abrupt shocks of reality. How much human misery and unrepeatable calamity lie hidden behind such words and phrases as "curtain fire", "local bombardment", "clashes of patrols", "strategic retreat", "heavy fighting", "advance held up", "aerial bombing", "casualties"! We cease to think of Jack, Jean, and Johann, and talk of Divisions and Corps. We even rejoice—it is horrible—at "enemy casualties". Delicate women look pleased when they hear that "the ground in front of our positions is heaped with enemy dead". And yet they are shocked by the simple-minded and practical cannibal who makes a meal of his enemy or his grandmother. We should not say, "as savage as a wild beast", but "as savage as civilized man". How can we look on ourselves and our species with anything but disgust?

from Life for Life's Sake by Richard Aldington

Peace

Now, God be thanked Who has matched us with His hour,
　And caught our youth, and wakened us from sleeping,
With hand made sure, clear eye, and sharpened power,
　To turn, as swimmers into cleanness leaping,
Glad from a world grown old and cold and weary,
　Leave the sick hearts that honour could not move,
And half-men, and their dirty songs and dreary,
　And all the little emptiness of love!

Oh! we, who have known shame, we have found release there,
　Where there's no ill, no grief, but sleep has mending,
　　Naught broken save this body, lost but breath;
Nothing to shake the laughing heart's long peace there
　But only agony, and that has ending;
　　And the worst friend and enemy is but Death.

Rupert Brooke

London: Sergeant with recruits

On August 3, 1914, I was a young schoolboy on my holidays, playing tennis in a set of mixed doubles. About five o'clock a paper-boy entered the tennis-club grounds with the *Evening News*. My male opponent, although he was serving, stopped his game for a minute and bought a paper.

"Hang the paper!" called I, indifferent to the fact that the Old World was falling about our ears and England's last day of peace was going down with the afternoon sun. "Your service. Love—fifteen."

"By Jove," he cried, after scanning the paper, "we're in!"

"What do you mean," cried the girls, "have the Germans declared war on us?"

"No. But we've sent an ultimatum to Germany which expires at twelve tonight. That means Britain will be in a state of war with Germany as from midnight." The hand that held the paper trembled with excitement.

"How frightfully thrilling!" said one girl.

"How awful!" whispered the other.

"How ripping!" corrected I. "Crash on with the game. Your service. Love—fifteen."

Five days later it was decided that I should not return to school, but should go at once into the army. So it was that I never finished up in the correct style at Kensingtowe with an emotional last chapel, endless good wishes and a lump in my throat. I just didn't go back.

Instead, an influential friend, who knew the old Colonel of the 2nd Tenth East Cheshires, a territorial battalion of my grandfather's regiment, secured for me and, at my request, for Doe commissions in that unit.

So one day we two trusty and well-beloved subjects, flushed, very nervous, and clad in the most expensive khaki uniforms that London could provide, took train for the North to interview the Colonel of the 2nd Tenth. He was sitting at a littered writing-table, when we were shown in by a smart orderly. We saw a plump old territorial Colonel, grey-haired, grey-moustached, and kindly in face. His khaki jacket was brightened by the two South African medal ribbons; and we were so sadly fresh to things military as to wonder whether either was the V.C. We saluted with great smartness, and hoped we had made the movement correctly: for really we knew very little about it. I wasn't sure whether we ought to salute indoors; and Doe, having politely bared his fair head on entering the office, saluted without a cap. I blushed at my bad manners and surreptitiously removed mine. Not knowing what to do with my hands, I put them in my pockets. I knew that, if something didn't happen quickly, I should start giggling. Here in the presence of our new commanding officer I felt as I used to when I stood before the head master.

"Sit down," beamed the C.O.

We sat down, crossed our legs, and tried to appear at our ease, and languid; as became officers.

"How old are you?" the Colonel asked Doe.

Doe hesitated, wondering whether to perjure himself and say "Twenty."

"Eighteen, sir," he admitted, obviously ashamed.

"And you, Ray?"

"Eighteen, sir," said I, feeling Doe's companion in guilt.

"Splendid, perfectly splendid!" replied the Colonel. "Eighteen, by Jove! You've timed your lives wonderfully, my boys. To be eighteen in 1914 is to be the best thing in England. England's wealth used to consist in other things. Nowadays you boys are the richest thing she's got. She's solvent with you, and bankrupt without you. Eighteen, confound it! It's a virtue to be your age, just as it's a crime to be mine. Now, look here"—the Colonel drew up his chair, as if he were going to get to business—"look here. Eighteen years ago you were born for this day. Through the last eighteen years you've been educated for it. Your birth and breeding were given you that you might officer England's youth in this hour. And now you enter upon your inheritance. Just as this is *the* day in the history of the world so yours is *the* generation. No other generation has been called to such grand things, and to such crowded, glorious living. Any other generation at your age would be footling around, living a shallow existence in the valleys, or just beginning to climb a slope to higher things. But you"—here the Colonel tapped the writing-table with his forefinger—"you, just because you've timed your lives aright, are going to be transferred straight to the mountain-tops. Well, I'm damned. Eighteen!"

4

I remember how his enthusiasm radiated from him and kindled a responsive excitement in me. I had entered his room a silly boy with no nobler thought than a thrill in the new adventure on which I had so suddenly embarked. But, as this fatherly old poet, touched by England's need and by the sight of two boys entering his room, so fresh and strong and ready for anything, broke into eloquence, I saw dimly the great ideas he was striving to express. I felt the brilliance of being alive in this big moment; the pride of youth and strength. I felt Aspiration surging in me and speeding up the action of my heart. I think I half hoped it would be my high lot to die on the battlefield.

"D'you see what I'm driving at?" asked the old Colonel.

"Rather!" answered Doe, with eagerness. Turning towards him as he spoke, I saw by the shining in his brown eyes that the poet in him had answered to the call of the old officer's words. His aspiration as well as mine was inflamed. Doe was feeling great. He was picturing himself, no doubt, leading a forlorn hope into triumph, or fighting a rearguard action and saving the British line. The heroic creature was going to be equal to the great moment and save England dramatically.

Pleased with Doe's ready understanding—my friend always captivated people in the first few minutes—our C.O. warmed still more to his subject. Having put his hands in his pockets and leant back in his chair to survey us the better, he continued:

"What I mean is—had you been eighteen a generation earlier, the British Empire could have treated you as very insignificant fry, whereas today she is obliged to come to you boys and say 'You take top place in my aristocracy. You're on top because I must place the whole weight of everything I have upon your shoulders. You're on top because you are the Capitalists, possessing an enormous capital of youth and strength and boldness and endurance. You must give it all to me—to gamble with—for my life. I've nothing to give you in return, except suffering and—' "

The Colonel paused, feeling he had said enough—or too much. We made no murmur of agreement. It would have seemed like applauding in church. Then he proceeded:

"Well, you're coming to my battalion, aren't you?"

"Yes, rather, sir," said Doe.

"Right. You're just the sort of boys that I want. If you're young and bold, your men will follow you anywhere. In this fight it's going to be better to be a young officer, followed and loved because of his youth, than to be an old one, followed and trusted because of his knowledge. Dammit! I wish I could make you see it. But, for God's sake, be enthusiastic. Be enthusiastic over the great crisis, over the responsibility, over your amazingly high calling."

He stopped, and began playing with a pencil; and it was some while before he added, speaking uncomfortably and keeping his eyes upon the pencil:

"Take a pride in your bodies, and hold them in condition. You'll want 'em. There are more ways than one of getting them tainted in the life of temptations you're going to face. I expect you—you grasp my meaning. . . . But, if only you'll light up your enthusiasm, everything else will be all right."

He raised his eyes and looked at us again, saying:

"Well, goodbye for the present."

We shook hands, saluted, and went out.

from *Tell England* by Ernest Raymond

Your King and Country Want You

O, we don't want to lose you But we think you ought to go, For your King and your coun-try Both need you so. We shall love you and miss you, But with all our might and main, We shall cheer you, thank you, kiss you, When you come home a-gain.

Paul Rubens

6

Fall In

What will you lack, sonny, what will you lack
When the girls line up the street,
Shouting their love to the lads come back
From the foe they rushed to beat?
Will you send a strangled cheer to the sky
And grin till your cheeks are red?
But what will you lack when your mate goes by
With a girl who cuts you dead?

Where will you look, sonny, where will you look
When your children yet to be
Clamour to learn of the part you took
In the war that kept men free?
Will you say it was naught to you if France
Stood up to her foe or bunked?
But where will you look when they give the glance
That tells you they know you funked?

How will you fare, sonny, how will you fare
In the far-off winter night,
When you sit by the fire in an old man's chair
And your neighbours talk of the fight?
Will you slink away, as it were from a blow,
Your old head shamed and bent?
Or—say I was not with the first to go,
But I went, thank God, I went?

Why do they call, sonny, why do they call
For men who are brave and strong?
Is it naught to you if your country fall,
And Right is smashed by Wrong?
Is it football still and the picture show,
The pub and betting odds,
When your brothers stand to the tyrant's blow
And England's call is God's?

Harold Begbie

"The mills of God grind slowly, but they grind exceeding small!" Aye, friend, and the slower they grind the smaller they crush. And that is why Kaiser William the Second—the Butcher of Berlin—will assuredly be crushed, utterly and for everlasting. . . .

Yes, that is his proper description—the Butcher of Berlin. All idea of German civilization has gone; it has been shattered for ever. . . . Take the sacking and destruction of Louvain—an open, undefended town in Brabant, which has hitherto been known to scholars throughout the world as the Oxford of Belgium. Its monuments, its university, its library, its stately churches, its priceless art treasures, have all been ruthlessly and wantonly destroyed by the brutal savages of the Kaiser. Henceforth, let the word "German" stand for the ideas which it will connote—vandalism, ignorance, brutality and cowardice—and, above all, for cowardice—for what can be more dastardly, more truly akin to the cruelty of the savage, than to wreak vengeance, after defeat, upon the innocent and the defenceless ? . . .

Then from all quarters, from Belgian refugees, from wounded British soldiers, from priests and burgomasters, come harrowing tales of the wounded being brutally killed, of women and children outraged and butchered—by a fiendish soldiery bent upon glutting its rage upon the defenceless victims placed at their mercy by the fortune of war. . . .

Such, then, is the nation—and such the Emperor—upon whom the vengeance of outraged humanity, invoking the great God of Battles, is about to descend. For the Godhead is a complex and all-embracing thing. There is no place in this bloody business for the God of Love; it is not *He* who works the slowly, surely grinding mills. Were it so, we should be saved the anguish of the slaughter of our own loved ones; there would be no widows' tears, no orphans' cries, no mothers' grief, no sisters' sorrow. The neck of the monster would go straight under the stones—and he would be no more. But not so with *this* God. *He* decrees that we, too, must see and taste of the bitterness—however righteous our cause. And therein lies the mystery. It is idle to attempt to penetrate it. Some day the veil may be lifted—and we shall see. And, seeing, we shall understand. Today, we grope in darkness, almost despairing of our race. But there, far ahead, we see the faint light of a New World; behind it we discern the outlines of the Prince of Peace; and, as we step warily, day by day, towards him, over and above all the din of battle—the roar of cannon, the clashing of swords, the cries of wounded, and the solemn silence of the dead—we are conscious of an awful, never-ceasing sound. And there, before the light, we at length see the Mills of God—grinding, grinding, grinding; and beneath them, beyond all hope of rescue or escape, there writhes a mad Teutonic tyrant, with blood-guilt upon his head, the greed of conquest on his lips, and the doom of a People on his soul.

Come, brother, let us turn our eyes to the light!

Editorial by Horatio Bottomley from *John Bull*, September 12th, 1914

Daddy, what did YOU do in the Great War?

Meanwhile, I was living at the highest possible emotional tension. Although I did not foresee anything like the full disaster of the War, I foresaw a great deal more than most people did. The prospect filled me with horror, but what filled me with even more horror was the fact that the anticipation of carnage was delightful to something like ninety per cent of the population. I had to revise my views on human nature. At that time I was wholly ignorant of psycho-analysis, but I arrived for myself at a view of human passions not unlike that of the psycho-analysts. I arrived at this view in an endeavour to understand popular feeling about the War. I had supposed until that time that it was quite common for parents to love their children, but the War persuaded me that it is a rare exception. I had supposed that most people liked money better than almost anything else, but I discovered that they liked destruction even better. I had supposed that intellectuals frequently loved truth, but I found here again that not ten per cent of them prefer truth to popularity. Gilbert Murray, who had been a close friend of mine since 1902, was a pro-Boer when I was not. I therefore naturally expected that he would again be on the side of peace; yet he went out of his way to write about the wickedness of the Germans, and the super-human virtue of Sir Edward Grey. I became filled with despairing tenderness towards the young men who were to be slaughtered, and with rage against all the statesmen of Europe. For several weeks I felt that if I should happen to meet Asquith or Grey I should be unable to refrain from murder. Gradually, however, these personal feelings disappeared. They were swallowed up by the magnitude of the tragedy, and by the realization of the popular forces which the statesmen merely let loose.

In the midst of this, I was myself tortured by patriotism. The successes of the Germans before the Battle of the Marne were horrible to me. I desired the defeat of Germany as ardently as any retired colonel. Love of England is very nearly the strongest emotion I possess, and in appearing to set it aside at such a moment, I was making a very difficult renunciation. Nevertheless, I never had a moment's doubt as to what I must do. I have at times been paralysed by scepticism, at times I have been cynical, at other times indifferent, but when the War came I felt as if I heard the voice of God. I knew that it was my business to protest, however futile protest might be. My whole nature was involved. As a lover of truth, the national propaganda of all the belligerent nations sickened me. As a lover of civilization, the return to barbarism appalled me. As a man of thwarted parental feeling, the massacre of the young wrung my heart. I hardly supposed that much good would come of opposing the War, but I felt that for the honour of human nature those who were not swept off their feet should show that they stood firm. After seeing troop trains departing from Waterloo, I used to have strange visions of London as a place of unreality. I used in imagination to see the bridges collapse and sink, and the whole great city vanish like a morning mist. Its inhabitants began to seem like hallucinations, and I would wonder whether the world in which I thought I had lived was a mere product of my own febrile nightmares. Such moods, however, were brief, and were put an end to by the need of work.

from Volume II of Bertrand Russell's Autobiography

Berlin: German soldiers leaving for the front, August 1914

Rendezvous

I have a rendezvous with Death
At some disputed barricade,
When Spring comes back with rustling shade
And apple blossoms fill the air—
I have a rendezvous with Death
When Spring brings back blue days and fair.

It may be he shall take my hand
And lead me into his dark land
And close my eyes and quench my breath—
It may be I shall pass him still.
I have a rendezvous with Death
On some scarred slope of battered hill,
When Spring comes round again this year
And the first meadow flowers appear.

God knows 'twere better to be deep
Pillowed in silk and scented down,
Where love throbs out in blissful sleep,
Pulse nigh to pulse, and breath to breath,

Where hushed awakenings are dear. . . .
But I've a rendezvous with Death
At midnight in some flaming town,
When Spring trips north again this year,
And I to my pledged word am true,
I shall not fail that rendezvous.

Alan Seeger

Guarding prisoners seemed an unheroic part to be playing in the war which, by October, had reached a critical stage; I wanted to be abroad fighting. My training had been interrupted, and I knew that even when recalled from detachment duty, I should have to wait a month or two at least before getting sent out. When I returned to the depot, "Tibs" Crawshay, the adjutant, a keen regular soldier, found two things wrong with me. First of all—I had not only gone to an inefficient tailor, but also had a soldier-servant who neglected to polish my buttons and shine my belt and boots as he should have done. Never having owned a valet before, I did not know what to expect of him. Crawshay finally summoned me to the Orderly Room. He would not send me to France, he said, until I had entirely over-hauled my wardrobe and looked more like a soldier—my company commander's report on me was "unsoldierlike and a nuisance". But my pay only just covered the mess bills, and I could hardly ask my parents to buy me another outfit so soon after assuring them that I had everything necessary. Crawshay next decided that I must be a poor sportsman—probably because on the day of the Grand National, in which a horse of his was running, all the young officers applied for leave to see the race, except myself. I volunteered to take the job of Orderly Officer for the Day for someone who wanted to go.

One by one my contemporaries were sent out to France to take the place of casualties in the First and Second Battalions, while I remained despondently at the depot. But again boxing helped me. Johnny Basham, a sergeant in the regiment, was training at the time for his fight—which he won—with Boswell for the Lonsdale Belt, welter-weight. I visited the training camp one evening, where Basham was offering to fight three rounds with any member of the regiment—the more the merrier. A young officer pulled on the gloves, and Basham got roars of laughter from the crowd as soon as he had taken his opponent's measure, by dodging around and playing the fool with him. I asked Basham's manager if I could have a go. He lent me some shorts, and I stepped into the ring. Pretending to know nothing of boxing, I led off with my right and moved clumsily. Basham saw a chance of getting another laugh; he dropped his guard and danced about with a you-can't-hit-me challenge. I caught him off his balance, and knocked him across the ring. He recovered and went for me, but I managed to keep on my feet. When I laughed at him, he laughed too. We had three very brisk rounds, and he very decently made me seem a much better boxer than I was, by accommodating his pace to mine. As soon as Crawshay heard the story, he rang me up at my billet and told me that he had learned with pleasure of my performance; that for an officer to box like that was a great encouragement for the men; that he was mistaken about my sportsmanship; and that, to show his appreciation, he would put me down for a draft to France in a week's time.

from *Goodbye to All That* by Robert Graves

[*This paper is to be considered by each soldier as confidential, and to be kept in his Active Service Pay Book.*]

You are ordered abroad as a soldier of the King to help our French comrades against the invasion of a common Enemy. You have to perform a task which will need your courage, your energy, your patience. Remember that the honour of the British Army depends on your individual conduct. It will be your duty not only to set an example of discipline and perfect steadiness under fire but also to maintain the most friendly relations with those whom you are helping in this struggle. The operations in which you are engaged will, for the most part, take place in a friendly country, and you can do your own country no better service than in showing yourself in France and Belgium in the true character of a British soldier.

Be invariably courteous, considerate and kind. Never do anything likely to injure or destroy property,

W15103—11592 100,000 2/17 HWV(P1177)

and always look upon looting as a disgraceful act. You are sure to meet with a welcome and to be trusted; your conduct must justify that welcome and that trust. Your duty cannot be done unless your health is sound. So keep constantly on your guard against any excesses. In this new experience you may find temptations both in wine and women. You must entirely resist both temptations, and, while treating all women with perfect courtesy, you should avoid any intimacy.

Do your duty bravely.
Fear God.
Honour the King.

KITCHENER,
Field-Marshal.

14

Goodbye-ee!

Good - bye-ee!__ good-bye-ee!__ Wipe the tear, ba - by dear, from your

eye-ee.__ Tho' it's hard to part, I know, I'll be

tick-led to death to go. Don't cry-ee!__ don't sigh-ee!__

There's a sil-ver lin-ing in the sky-ee.__ Bon-soir, old thing! cheer-i-

o! chin-chin! Nah-poo! Too-dle-oo! Good-bye-ee!__

R. P. Weston and Bert Lee

The Parable of the Old Man and the Young

So Abram rose, and clave the wood, and went,
And took the fire with him, and a knife.
And as they sojourned both of them together,
Isaac the first-born spake and said, My Father,
Behold the preparations, fire and iron,
But where the lamb for this burnt-offering?
Then Abram bound the youth with belts and straps,
And builded parapets and trenches there,
And stretchèd forth the knife to slay his son.
When lo! an angel called him out of heaven,
Saying, Lay not thy hand upon the lad,
Neither do anything to him. Behold,
A ram, caught in a thicket by its horns;
Offer the Ram of Pride instead of him.
But the old man would not so, but slew his son,
And half the seed of Europe, one by one.

Wilfred Owen

The great "Business as Usual" phase was already passing away, and London was in the full tide of recruiting enthusiasm. That tide was breaking against the most miserable arrangements for enlistment it is possible to imagine. Overtaxed and not very competent officers, whose one idea of being very efficient was to refuse civilian help and be very, very slow and circumspect and very dignified and overbearing, sat in dirty little rooms and snarled at this unheard-of England that pressed at door and window for enrolment. Outside every recruiting office crowds of men and youths waited, leaning against walls, sitting upon the pavements, waited for long hours, waiting to the end of the day and returning next morning, without shelter, without food, many sick with hunger; men who had hurried up from the country, men who had thrown up jobs of every kind, clerks, shopmen, anxious only to serve England and "teach those damned Germans a lesson". Between them and this object they had discovered a perplexing barrier; an inattention. As Mr. Britling made his way by St. Martin's Church and across Trafalgar Square and marked the weary accumulation of this magnificently patriotic stuff, he had his first inkling of the imaginative insufficiency of the War Office that had been so suddenly called upon to organize victory. He was to be more fully informed when he reached his club. . . .

The prevailing topic in the smoking-room upstairs was the inability of the War Office to deal with the flood of recruits that was pouring in, and its hostility to any such volunteering as Mr. Britling had in mind. Quite a number of members wanted to volunteer; there was much talk of their fitness; "I'm fifty-four," said one, "and I could do my twenty-five miles in marching kit far better than half those boys of nineteen." Another was thirty-eight. "I must hold the business together," he said; "but why anyhow shouldn't I learn to shoot and use a bayonet?" The personal pique of the rejected lent force to their criticisms of the recruiting and general organization. "The War Office has one incurable system," said a big mine-owner. "During peace time it runs all its home administration with men who will certainly be wanted at the front directly there is a war. Directly war comes, therefore, there is a shift all round, and a new untried man—usually a dug-out in an advanced state of decay—is stuck into the job. Chaos follows automatically. The War Office always has done this, and so far as one can see it always will. It seems incapable of realizing that another man will be wanted until the first is taken away. Its imagination doesn't even run to that."

Mr. Britling found a kindred spirit in Wilkins.

Wilkins was expounding his tremendous scheme for universal volunteering. Everybody was to be accepted. Everybody was to be assigned and registered and—*badged*.

"A brassard," said Mr. Britling.

"It doesn't matter whether we really produce a fighting force or not," said Wilkins. "Everybody now is enthusiastic—and serious. Everybody is willing to put on some kind of uniform and submit to some sort of orders. And the thing to do is to catch them in the willing stage. Now is the time to get the country lined up and organized, ready to meet the internal stresses that are bound to come later. But there's no disposition whatever to welcome this universal offering. It's just as though this war was a treat to which only the very select friends of the War Office were to be admitted. And I don't admit that the national volunteers would be ineffective—even from a military point of view. There are plenty of fit men of our age, and men of proper age who are better employed at home—armament workers for example, and there are all the boys under the age. They may not be under the age before things are over. . . ."

He was even prepared to plan uniforms.

"A brassard," repeated Mr. Britling, "and perhaps coloured strips on the revers of a coat."

"Colours for the counties," said Wilkins, "and if there isn't coloured cloth to be got there's—red flannel. Anything is better than leaving the mass of people to mob about. . . ."

A momentary vision danced before Mr. Britling's eyes of red flannel petticoats being torn up in a rapid improvisation of soldiers to resist a sudden invasion. Passing washerwomen suddenly requisitioned. But one must not let oneself be laughed out of good intentions because of ridiculous accessories. The idea at any rate was the sound one. . . .

The vision of what ought to be done shone brightly while Mr. Britling and Mr. Wilkins maintained it. But presently under discouraging reminders that there were no rifles, no instructors, and, above all, the open hostility of the established authorities, it faded again. . . .

Afterwards in other conversations Mr. Britling reverted to more modest ambitions.

"Is there no clerical work, no minor administrative work, a man might be used for ?" he asked.

"Any old dug-out," said the man with the thin face, "any old doddering Colonel Newcome, is preferred to you in that matter. . . ."

Mr. Britling emerged from his club about half-past three with his mind rather dishevelled and with his private determination to do something promptly for his country's needs blunted by a perplexing "How ?" His search for doors and ways where no doors and ways existed went on with a gathering sense of futility.

He had a ridiculous sense of pique at being left out, like a child shut out from a room in which a vitally interesting game is being played.

"After all, it is *our* war," he said.

from *Mr. Britling Sees It Through* by H. G. Wells

Fred Karno's Army

We are Fred Karno's Army,
The rag-time infantry:
We cannot fight, we cannot shoot,
What bleedin' use are we ?
And when we get to Berlin,
The Kaiser he will say,
Hoch! Hoch!! mein Gott,
What a bloody rotten lot
Are the rag-time infantry.

Sung to the tune of *The Church's One Foundation*

New Army Education

I learned to wash in shell-holes, and to shave myself in tea,
While the fragments of a mirror did a balance on my knee.
I learned to dodge the whizzbangs and the flying lumps of lead,
And to keep a foot of earth between the snipers and my head.
I learned to keep my haversack well-filled with buckshee food,
To take my army issue and to pinch what else I could.
I learned to cook maconachie with candle-ends and string,
With four-by-two and sardine oil, and any old darn thing.
I learned to use my bayonet according as you please,
For a bread-knife or a chopper, or a prong for toasting cheese.
I learned to gather souvenirs that home I hoped to send,
And hump them round for months and months, and dump them
   in the end.
I never used to grumble after breakfast in the line
That the eggs were cooked too lightly or the bacon cut too fine.
I never told a sergeant just exactly what I thought,
I never did a pack drill, for I never quite got caught.
I never stopped a whizzbang, though I've stopped a lot of mud;
But the one that Fritz sent over with my name on was a dud.

Anon.

The trench system has one thing to recommend it. It tidies things
up a bit.

For the first few months after the war broke out confusion reigned
supreme. Belgium and the north of France were one huge jumbled
battlefield, rather like a public park on a Saturday afternoon—one
of those parks where promiscuous football is permitted. Friend and
foe were inextricably mingled, and the direction of the goal was
uncertain. . . . There was no front and no rear, so direction counted
for nothing. The country swarmed with troops which had been left
"in the air", owing to their own too rapid advance, or the equally
rapid retirement of their supporters; with scattered details trying to

rejoin their units; or with despatch-riders hunting for a peripatetic Divisional Headquarters. Snipers shot both sides impartially. It was all most upsetting.

Well, as already indicated, the trench system has put all that right. The trenches now run continuously—a long, irregular, but perfectly definite line of cleavage—from the North Sea to the Vosges. Everybody has been carefully sorted out—human beings on one side, Germans on the other. . . .

The result is an agreeable blend of war and peace. This week, for instance, our battalion has been undergoing a sort of rest-cure a few miles from the hottest part of the firing line. (We had a fairly heavy spell of work last week.) In the morning we wash our clothes, and perform a few mild martial exercises. In the afternoon we sleep, in all degrees of *déshabillé*, under the trees in an orchard. In the evening we play football, or bathe in the canal, or lie on our backs on the grass, watching our aeroplanes buzzing home to roost, attended by German shrapnel. We could not have done this in the autumn. Now, thanks to our trenches, a few miles away, we are as safe here as in the wilds of Argyllshire or West Kensington.

But there are drawbacks to everything. The fact is, a trench is that most uninteresting of human devices, a compromise. It is neither satisfactory as a domicile nor efficient as a weapon of offence. The most luxuriant dug-out; the most artistic window-box—these, in spite of all biassed assertions to the contrary, compare unfavourably with a flat in Knightsbridge. On the other hand, the knowledge that you are keeping yourself tolerably immune from the assaults of your enemy is heavily discounted by the fact that the enemy is equally immune from yours. In other words, you "get no forrarder" with a trench; and the one thing which we are all anxious to do out here is to bring this war to a speedy and gory conclusion, and get home to hot baths and regular meals.

So a few days ago we were not at all surprised to be informed officially that trench life is to be definitely abandoned, and Hun-hustling to begin in earnest.

from The First Hundred Thousand by Ian Hay

No. 1 section were already moving off, he fell in behind, and followed on. Slowly they made progress along the traverses, more easy to negotiate by light of day. Not night-bred fear, nor dark mystification nor lurking unseen snares any longer harassed them, but instead, a penetrating tedium, a boredom that leadened and oppressed, making the spirit quail and tire, took hold of them, as they went to their first fatigue. The untidied squalor of the loveless scene spread far horizontally, imaging unnamed discomfort, sordid and deprived as ill-kept hen-runs that back on sidings on wet weekdays where waste-land meets environs and punctured bins ooze canned-meats discarded, tyres to rot, derelict slow-weathered ironware disintegrates between factory-end and nettle-bed. Sewage feeds the high grasses and bald clay-crop bears tins and braces, swollen rat-body turned-turtle to the clear morning.

Men-bundles here and there in ones and twos, in twos and threes; some eating, others very still, knee to chin trussed, confined in small dug concavities, wombed of earth, their rubber-sheets for caul. Others coaxed tiny smouldering fires, balancing precarious mess-tins, anxious-watched to boil. Rain clouds gathered and returned with the day's progression, with the west wind freshening. The south-west wind caught their narrow gullies in enfilade, gusting about every turn of earth-work, lifting dripping ground-sheets, hung to curtain little cubby-holes. All their world shelving, coagulate. Under-earth shorn-up, seeled and propt. Substantial matter guttered and dissolved, sprawled to glaucous insecurity. All sureness metamorphosed, all slippery a place for the children of men, for the fair feet of us to go up and down in.

It was mild for the time of year, what they call a Green Christmas.

They spoke words of recognition where familiar faces poked out from bivvy-sheets, where eyes peered from dark hovel-holes, flimsy-roofed with corrugated-iron. They gained information, in their passing, of the state of the war as it affected "A" Company, which brought little additional data to their own observations—it appeared to be equally cushy on the whole half-battalion frontage. They passed a point where the fire-trench cut the pavé road, the road of last night's itinerary. They passed where an angled contrivance of breast-works formed a defensive passage, a cunning opening east-ward, opening outward, a sally-way; a place of significance to drawers up of schemes, a pin-point of the front-system known to the Staff.

No. 1 section seemed the only unfortunates stirring. All things were very still, universally wet wrapt; this sodden silence might have been from eternity unchanging, seemed a timeless act of fluid dissolution.

They reached a place where the high walls of the communication trench considerably contracted at a turn, reducing the strip of sky above them. These reeking sack walls block all lateral view, and above, nothing is visible save the rain-filmed, narrowing ribbon of sky.

Men sensitive of hearing cock heads enquiringly, as rodents aware, prick ears, acutely directed suddenly.

The narrow air where they walked, registered in quick succession, a series of distinct, far over, separately discerned, vibrations; and after the drawing of a breath—for the balmy morning, for the damp inertia: delved plungings boring to the root of things.

High-powered, of sure trajectory, that big bugger stopt short, with so oddly insignificant a thud, yet to upheavals of earth and water. The dug place in whose depth they sheltered shockt and tremored with each projectile's violent nosing, whether of dud or lively detonate.

Their progress was without event; here and there the trench was lower built or not so repaired from damage, and they momentarily had view of where a continuing double line of trees masked the passage of a road, parallel to where they went securely in the trench; the road they walked on in the darkness of the night before.

Most of them failed to recognize this landmark and were at a loss as to their position and precise direction, except that they supposed themselves to be making for Sandbag Alley, that long circuitous corridor of last night's gropings. They felt only the maze-likeness of all their goings, being aware of nothing much more than the approximate direction of the enemy line. As when you come toward the sea and are conscious of her, and know vaguely the direction you must take for your eyes to see her, yet are in ignorance of the crooked by-streets to and from the jetty.

They met no one on their way and said few words to each other. It must have been a quarter of an hour before they halted where a tramway cut the trench. The continuing rain came softly, in even descent, percolating all things through.

A low shelter stood, its galvanized inclining roof reflecting the sky's leaden, resounded to the water-pelter, each corrugation a separate gully, a channel for the flow. The trench-drain, disintegrated, fallen-in before the strong current it was built to canalize. Aquatic suckings betrayed where some tiny trickling found new vent-way for the rising inundation.

Corporal Quilter made investigation round and about the lean-to. No human being was visible in the trench or on the open track. A man, seemingly native to the place, a little thick man, swathed with sacking, a limp, saturated bandolier thrown over one shoulder and with no other accoutrements, gorgeted in woollen Balaclava, groped out from between two tottering corrugated uprights, his great moustaches beaded with condensation under his nose. Thickly greaved with mud so that his boots and puttees and sandbag tie-ons were become one whole of trickling ochre. His minute pipe had its smoking bowl turned inversely. He spoke slowly. He told the corporal that this was where shovels were usually drawn for any fatigue in the supports. He slipped back quickly, with a certain animal caution, into his hole; to almost immediately poke out his wool-work head, to ask if anyone had the time of day or could spare him some dark shag or a picture-paper. Further, should they meet a white dog in the trench her name was Belle, and he would like to catch any bastard giving this Belle the boot.

John Ball told him the time of day.

No one had any dark shag.

No one had a picture-paper.

They certainly would be kind to the bitch, Belle. They'd give her half their iron rations—Jesus—they'd let her bite their backsides without a murmur.

He draws-to the sacking curtain over his lair.

Corporal Quilter beckoned his men to where a series of disused fire-bays led from the main trench.

Picks, shovels, dredging-ladles, carriers, containers, gas-rattles, two of Mrs. Thingumajig's patent gas-dispersing flappers, emptied

S.A.A. boxes, grenade boxes, two bales of revetting-wire, pine stakes; rusted-to-bright-orange barbed wire of curious design—three coils of it; fine good new dark efficient corkscrew staples, splayed-out all ways; three drums of whale oil, the splintered stock of a Mauser rifle, two unexploded yellow-ochre toffee-apples, their strong rods unrusted; three left-leg gum-boots; a Scotch officer's fine bright bonnet; some type of broken pump, its rubber slack punctured, coiled like a dead slime-beast, reared its brass nozzle out from under rum-jar and picket-maul.

This trove piled haphazardly, half-submerged. You must have a lumber room where you have habitation.

Corporal Quilter calls the leading man. He indicates with a jerk of the head the job of work.

One and one, from one pair of hands to another equally reluctant, they pass the shovels the length of the file.

Corporal Quilter stands watching.

There wanted one shovel to the number of the party. Private Saunders devised that he should be the unprovided man, by the expedient of busying himself with his left puttee, conveniently come down.

Corporal Quilter spits from time to time on the duck-board. He hands to Private Saunders a dredging-ladle and the heavier pick, the other he takes himself. He gives the word of command to move on.

The warden of stores withdraws again his curtain; his shiny threadbare hindparts first thrust out—now his whole hair-suit torso, now his aboriginal mask.

N.C.O. in charge of party—you corporal.

Corporal Quilter signatures the chit.

> 12 shovels
> 2 picks
> 1 ladle

See yer bring 'em again—all the so-called complement.

They watched him vanish, mandrill fashion, into his enclosure. They wondered how long a time it took to become so knit with the texture of this countryside, so germane to the stuff about, so moulded by, made proper to, the special environment dictated by a stationary war.

from In Parenthesis by David Jones

I Want to Go Home

I want to go home, _____ I want to go home, _____ I don't want to go to the trench-es no more Where whizz-bangs and shrap-nel they whis-tle and roar. Take me ov - er the sea _____ Where the Al - ley - man can't get at me. _____ Oh, my! I don't want to die, I want to go home. _____

Lt. Gitz Rice

To see the devastation wrought by last night's air raid unaccustomed visitors came flocking to the East End—well-dressed people in motors, journalists, photographers, high military officials, Red Cross nurses, policewomen, travellers from all over the world. . . .

Today these mean streets were thronged and seething. Poor people in frowzy garments crowded the roadways and squeezed past each other in the narrow alleys. What sights for the pretty ladies in dainty dresses, craning their slender white throats from taxi-cab windows! What sights for the rather too generously fed business men and well-groomed officers: miserable dwellings, far from fit for human families, poorly dressed women of working sort, with sad, worn faces; and others, sunk lower, just covered, no more, in horrid rags, hopeless, unhappy beings; half-clad neglected little children—sadder these even than the havoc wrought by German bombs! . . .

Crowds mostly made up of women gathered before each ruined home. One, where a child had been killed, was still inhabited. A soldier in khaki stood at the door striving in vain to keep back the press of human bodies surging against it. The people who lived there were scarcely able to force a way to their own door. A bomb had descended upon a brewery; from the roof to the cellar all had fallen, only the outer walls remained, and a mass of charred wood in the basement. Many dwellings were thus completely gutted. In the ashes left by the fires which had ravaged them nothing save the twisted ironwork of the bedsteads could be identified. A chorus of wailing stirred amongst the women: "Oh, my God! Look at the home!" . . .

Rumour raced hot-foot: "There were little lights signalling: telling them where to drop the bombs!" . . . "Germans!" . . . "Beasts." . . . "Germans!" . . . "I saw taxicabs driving up and down signalling!" . . . "Germans!" . . .

"They should all have been cleared out at the beginning of the war!" . . . "The Government has nowhere to put them!" . . . "They go and give themselves up to the police and they tell them to go home. . . . Everywhere a bomb is dropped you'll find one of their shops was wrecked near!"

Alas, where in the East End would one fail to find a German shop which had been wrecked in the anti-German riots? Near to the brewery was a baker's shop with a German name on the fascia; the door, the shutters, the very window-frames had been torn off. It was boarded up now with new, unpainted wood. The crowds as they passed it growled imprecations; wild stories grew there.

In Hoxton Street was a rush of excitement. A German baker's, one of the few still remaining, had just been raided. "They were serving bread there an hour ago!" a surprised voice uttered. "They go in to buy bread from them, and then they wreck the shop," another answered. The windows were smashed, only a few jagged bits of glass still attached to the framework. The pavement was littered with glass and flour. The shop had been cleared of everything portable. A policeman stood at the door. Two soldiers came out laughing. "There is plenty of new bread downstairs if you want

it; it will only be wasted there!" they called as they went off seeking
new quarry.

Down the street police whistles sounded vociferously: a babel of
shouting, tremendous outcry. A crowd was advancing at a run, a
couple of lads on bicycles leading, a swarm of children on the
fringes, screaming like gulls. Missiles were flying. In the centre of
the turmoil men dragged a big, stout man, stumbling and resisting
in their grasp, his clothes whitened by flour, his mouth dripping
blood. They rushed him on. New throngs closed round him.

From another direction arose more shouting. A woman's scream.
The tail of the crowd dashed off towards the sound. Crowds raced
to it from all directions . . . fierce, angry shouts and yells. . . .

A woman was in the midst of a struggling mob; her blouse half-
torn off, her fair hair fallen, her face contorted with pain and terror,
blood running down her bare white arm. A big, drunken man flung
her to the ground. She was lost to sight. . . . "Oh, my God! Oh!
They are kicking her!" a woman screamed.

"Do help her!" I pleaded with a soldier who stood watching. He
shrugged his shoulders. "I can't do anything." "You are a soldier;
they will respect you!" "Why should I ?" he asked with a curl of the
lip. "Look, there's another soldier; can't you get on to *him* ?"

"She is covered with blood!" a woman's voice cried again. I
struggled to reach her, but the closely packed onlookers would not
make way for me. An Army motor drove up and was halted by the
press. An officer, hawk-eyed, aquiline, sat in the front; there were
vacant seats behind. I sprang to the step: "A woman is being hurt
here. Will you take her away from the crowd?" "I don't think we
can: we are on military business," he answered curtly. The horn
was sounded, the people made way, the car drove on. . . .

The woman on the ground was unconscious. Those who a
moment before had shrieked imprecations were seized with pity.
The nearest raised her and rested her on a fruiterer's upturned
barrel. A couple of women supported her with their arms; another
was fastening up her hair. She drooped, still nerveless, her colour
gone, her eyes closed. They chafed her hands, the crowd about them
silent and awed. Passion was spent.

from *The Home Front* by Sylvia Pankhurst

FOR AUCTION
ANNOUNCEMENTS
See Page TEN.

Daily Express

NO. 4,706.   LONDON, SATURDAY, MAY 8, 1915.   ONE HALFPENNY.

BRAND'S
MEAT LOZENGES

The World's Greatest and Foulest Crime.

NO WARNING GIVEN.

LUSITANIA TORPEDOED & SUNK IN EIGHT MINUTES.

WAS THERE A CONVOY?

QUESTIONS RAISED BY THE GREAT DISASTER.

GREAT LINER GOES DOWN IN EIGHT MINUTES.

GRAVE MESSAGES.

BETWEEN 500 AND 600 SURVIVORS LANDED AT QUEENSTOWN.

MANY HOSPITAL CASES.

SPEED AND ROUTES.

STOPPING TO PICK UP A PILOT.

RUNNING RISKS.

German piracy reached its climax yesterday when the great Cunard liner Lusitania, with 1,978 souls on board, was sunk without warning by a submarine twenty-three miles west of Queenstown.

Up to a late hour last night only the scantiest details of the outrage had been received in London. Between 500 and 600 survivors, many of whom were injured and were taken to hospital, were landed last night at Queenstown. Some others have been landed at Kinsale. As the liner sank eight minutes after she was torpedoed there may have been considerable loss of life. Many prominent persons had booked passages in the Lusitania, including Mr. Charles Frohman, Mr. Alfred Vanderbilt, Mr. D. A. Thomas, Sir Hugh Lane, Lady Mackworth, and Lady Allan, wife of Sir Hugh Allan, of Montreal.

While the incident may impress the imagination by reason of the size of the liner, it will in no degree impair the courage of the nation, and will not have the slightest effect on the course of the war. It is simply an act of piracy and nothing more.

The Lusitania left New York on Saturday last with passengers and mails for Liverpool. Just before she sailed the German Embassy, on instructions from Berlin, published in the New York newspapers a warning to travellers that they embarked in British liners at their own risk. Anonymous warnings were also sent to persons who had booked berths, but little attention was paid to these communications, and the number of passengers created a record for the time of the year. There were on board:—First Class Passengers, 290; Second Class Passengers, 662; Third Class Passengers, 361; Crew, 665. Total, 1,978.

The first indication that the Germans might attempt to carry their threat into effect was afforded on Thursday afternoon by the presence of an enemy submarine in Dunmanus Bay, next to Bantry Bay, on the south-west coast of County Cork and ninety miles west of Queenstown. The submarine came close to the shore, and, having manoeuvred on the surface for some time, dived and was not seen again. Rumours were current in the City yesterday afternoon that the Lusitania had been attacked, and at 5.30 the Admiralty announced that she had been torpedoed and sunk off the Head of Kinsale, south of County Cork. Soon after the news became known in London the offices of the Cunard Company in Cockspur-street were besieged by friends of passengers, including many Americans, and expressions of indignation were heard on every hand. In New York the news caused intense excitement, and the stock market collapsed, all stocks falling from 5 to 10 points.

During the day it became known that two other large Liverpool steamers had been sunk, in St. George's Channel on Thursday by German submarines. They were the Candidate, of 5,858 tons, bound for Jamaica, and the Centurion, of 5,945 tons, bound for Durban.

CAPTAIN TURNER

MAP SHOWING THE SCENE OF THE DISASTER.

28

In judging of the attitude taken by the troops of the XII Corps in the face of the action of the civil population, which was hostile to the last degree and employed the most reprehensible methods, we must remember that the tactical aim of the XII Corps was the rapid passage over the Meuse and the clearing of the enemy from the left bank. The speedy suppression of the resistance of the inhabitants, which was directly opposed to this aim, was a military necessity to be secured by all possible means. From this point of view, the bombardment of the town, which was taking an active part in the fighting, and the burning of the houses occupied by the francs-tireurs, as well as the shooting of inhabitants caught with weapons in their hands, were all justified.

In the same way, the shooting of the hostages in various localities was also justified. The troops fighting in the town found themselves in the direst extremity, inasmuch as they were under the artillery, machine-gun, and rifle fire of the regular troops posted on the left bank of the Meuse, and were at the same time being fired at in the rear and on the flanks by the inhabitants. The hostages were taken as security in order to put a stop to the conduct of the francs-tireurs. Despite this, and since the population continued, as before, to inflict losses on the struggling troops, the shooting of the hostages was carried out; otherwise, the holding of the hostages would have only implied an empty threat. Their execution was all the more justified, since, with the general participation of the populace in the fighting, it was hardly a case of innocent victims. The lives of women and children were, on principle, spared, so long as they were not caught in the act, or it was not a case of self-defence against their attacks. . . .

Without doubt it is deeply regrettable that, in consequence of the events of August 23rd and 24th, the flourishing town of Dinant with its suburbs was burnt and laid in ruins and a great number of human lives were destroyed. The responsibility for this lies not on the German Army, but only on the population. The inhabitants collectively engaged in conflict with the German troops contrary to international law and in a fanatical and treacherous manner, and forced our troops to take those counter-measures required for the purposes of war.

Had the population held aloof from armed resistance and open participation in the fighting, scarcely any injury would have been incurred by them, as regards life or property, despite the hazardous position in which they were placed by reason of military operations.

BERLIN, *April 11th*, 1915.

Military Department of Investigation into the Violation of the Laws of War.

> Signed: Major BAUER.
> Signed: Councillor of the Supreme Court of
> Judicature, Dr. WAGNER.

from German Government Publication *The German Army in Belgium*

Battery Moving Up to a New Position from Rest Camp: Dawn

> Not a sign of life we rouse
> In any square close-shuttered house
> That flanks the road we amble down
> Toward far trenches through the town.
>
> The dark, snow-slushy, empty street. . . .
> Tingle of frost in brow and feet. . . .
> Horse-breath goes dimly up like smoke.
> No sound but the smacking stroke
>
> As a sergeant flings each arm
> Out and across to keep him warm,
> And the sudden splashing crack
> Of ice-pools broken by our track.
>
> More dark houses, yet no sign
> Of life. . . . And axle's creak and whine. . . .
> The splash of hooves, the strain of trace. . . .
> Clatter: we cross the market place.

Deep quiet again, and on we lurch
Under the shadow of a church:
Its tower ascends, fog-wreathed and grim;
Within its aisles a light burns dim. . . .

When, marvellous! from overhead,
Like abrupt speech of one deemed dead,
Speech-moved by some Superior Will,
A bell tolls thrice and then is still.

And suddenly I know that now
The priest within, with shining brow,
Lifts high the small round of the Host.
The server's tingling bell is lost

In clash of the greater overhead.
Peace like a wave descends, is spread,
While watch the peasants' reverent eyes. . . .
The bell's boom trembles, hangs, and dies.

O people who bow down to see
The Miracle of Calvary,
The bitter and the glorious,
Bow down, bow down and pray for us.

Once more our anguished way we take
Towards our Golgotha, to make
For all our lovers sacrifice.
Again the troubled bell tolls thrice.

And slowly, slowly, lifted up
Dazzles the overflowing cup.
O worshipping, fond multitude,
Remember us too, and our blood.

Turn hearts to us as we go by,
Salute those about to die,
Plead for them, the deep bell toll:
Their sacrifice must soon be whole.

Entreat you for such hearts as break
With the premonitory ache
Of bodies, whose feet, hands, and side,
Must soon be torn, pierced, crucified.

Sue for them and all of us
Who the world over suffer thus,
Who have scarce time for prayer indeed,
Who only march and die and bleed.

*　　*　　*　　*　　*

The town is left, the road leads on,
Bluely glaring in the sun,
Toward where in the sunrise gate
Death, honour, and fierce battle wait.

Robert Nichols

This Muddy War
"These 'ere staff cars do splash a lot, don't they Bill?" (No answer.)

The General

"Good-morning; good-morning!" the General said
When we met him last week on our way to the line.
Now the soldiers he smiled at are most of 'em dead,
And we're cursing his staff for incompetent swine.
"He's a cheery old card," grunted Harry to Jack
As they slogged up to Arras with rifle and pack.

* * * * *

But he did for them both by his plan of attack.

Siegfried Sassoon

Raining, Raining, Raining

Raining, raining, raining, always bloody well raining.
Raining all the morning, and raining all the day.
Grousing, grousing, grousing, always bloody well grousing.
Grousing at the weather, and grousing at the pay.

Sung to the tune of Holy, Holy, Holy!

Mud: an ammunition limber on the Flers–Les Boeufs road, November 1916

The communication trench was one of the longest that we ever used, and in many places it was bricked, sides and floor. It ended in a singular front line, approached by too many boyaux, known by their numbers; a front line not unhappily sited, but dominated by the enemy's higher ground, on which rose Auchy's crowding red roofs. Our company's notch of this front line was a deep trench, passing every twenty or thirty yards under roofs of iron rails or duckboards covered with sandbags. And this trench had been kept elegantly clean. On the wrong side of it, their mouths facing the German line, were several deep dugouts; forward from it reached several saps, chalky grooves which were by no means so tidy. And, not without their awe to the unaccustomed, there were mine-shafts in the line, mostly with wooden barriers and notices excluding infantry. "Keep Out. This Means You," was seen here.

The reason for the overhead coverings did not long keep me in suspense. It was my turn of trench watch, one grey morning; I walked to our left-hand post, and talked to our sentry there, when *whizz-crunch, whizz-crunch,* two small trench mortar shells of the kind called "pine-apples" fell on the covering above us, broke it half down and strewed the place with fragments. The immediateness of these arrivals annulled fear. Taking my meditative way along to the other extremity of our trench, I was genially desired by Corporal Worley to take cocoa with him; he was just bringing it to the boil over some shreds of sandbag and tallow candle. Scarcely had I grasped the friendly mug when a rifle-grenade burst fizzing on the parapet behind me and another on the parados behind him; and we were unhit. Worley's courtesy and warm feeling went on, undiverted as though a butterfly or two had settled on a flower.

The tunnellers who were so busy under the German line were men of stubborn determination, yet (by force of the unaccustomed) they hurried nervously along the trenches above ground to spend their long hours listening or mining. At one shaft they pumped air down with Brobdingnagian bellows. The squeaking noise may have given them away, or it may have been mere bad luck, when one morning a minenwerfer smashed this entrance and the men working there. One was carried out past me, collapsing like a sack of

potatoes, spouting blood at twenty places. Cambrin was beginning
to terrify. Not far away from that shafthead, a young and cheerful
lance-corporal of ours was making some tea as I passed one warm
afternoon. I went along three firebays; one shell burst behind me;
I saw its smoke faint out, and I thought all was as lucky as it should
be. Soon a cry from that place recalled me; the shell had burst all
wrong. Its butting impression was black and stinking in the parados
where three minutes ago the lance-corporal's mess-tin was bubbling
over a little flame. For him, how could the gobbets of blackening
flesh, the earth-wall sotted with blood, with flesh, the eye under the
duckboard, the pulpy bone be the only answer? At this moment,
while we looked with intense fear at so strange a horror, the lance-
corporal's brother came round the traverse.

He was sent to company headquarters in a kind of catalepsy. The
bay had to be put right, and Sergeant Simmons, having helped
himself and me to a share of rum, shovelled into the sandbag I held,
not without self-protecting profanity, and an air of "it's a lie;
we're a lie." Cambrin was beginning to terrify.

from Undertones of War by Edmund Blunden

The Morning Before the Battle

Today, the fight: my end is very soon,
    And sealed the warrant limiting my hours:
I knew it walking yesterday at noon
    Down a deserted garden full of flowers.
. . . Carelessly sang, pinned roses on my breast,
    Reached for a cherry-bunch—and then, then, Death
Blew through the garden from the north and east
    And blighted every beauty with chill breath.

I looked, and ah my wraith before me stood,
    His head all battered in by violent blows:
The fruit between my lips to clotted blood
    Was transubstantiate, and the pale rose
Smelt sickly, till it seemed through a swift tear-flood
    That dead men blossomed in the garden-close.

Robert Graves

Phillip followed the man in front. The centre company was already taking up its position in the dead ground through the trees. "B" Company passed behind them.

The advance was to be made in three lines, with the men extended to five paces. It took about ten nervous minutes to deploy.

"B" Company's position was on the right flank, in the second line. While Phillip waited behind an oak tree at the verge of the wood, he tried again to load his rifle. This time, the leading cartridge jammed. He wrenched back the bolt, the brass cartridge flipped out; he rammed back the bolt. The next cartridge stuck again. He struck it with his fist, uttering a wild cry: the tip of the nickel bullet broke off.

"I can't load my rifle!" he complained, as though to the tree. No one else took any notice of him; no one heard him. He tried once more, without success. Then looking at the next man, Elliott, he saw that he too was fumbling with his bolt. Sergeant Henshaw came running up. Phillip waited for him to pass, while trying to think of what to say. Shells were plunging down into the wood, with the noise of electric trams stopping in the High Street, only a thousand times darker, coarser. He heard distant shouts, the blowing of whistles. As "Grannie" Henshaw approached, he saw that his nostrils were distended. Beads of sweat glistened on his forehead.

"Sergeant—"

"Grannie" Henshaw took no notice. Phillip caught hold of his tunic. A face, no longer that of "Grannie" Henshaw, turned to him and cried, "I can't listen to anything now!" Then, with hand to ear, he stopped, looking towards Mr. Ogilby.

"Fix bayonets! Fix bayonets, everyone! Fix bayonets!" shouted "Grannie" Henshaw. Phillip saw officers drawing their swords.

Nearer whistles were blowing. Captain Forbes and Mr. Ogilby were swinging their arms for the advance. Phillip stood by the tree, as he fixed bayonet, "Grannie" Henshaw muttering to himself as he fixed his.

"Please, Sergeant, really, my rifle is no good! I can't load it!"

"It's the same with everybody else! You must load singly. Don't you ever listen to orders? Now go forward, like a good boy, and do what you're told!"

With a lingering glance at the tree, as to a friend he must leave for ever, Phillip made himself walk forward with the others, like a man walking through ice giving way before him. With shaking fingers he took a clip of five cartridges from a pouch and wrenched off one. Where to put the other four? For a few moments it was an imponderable problem. Then he thought of his right-hand lower tunic pocket. But it was already full—Civic, matches, pouch, bundle of letters from Mother. With a sob he tore at the contents of the pocket, trying to wrench away a fistful. He threw all away as though his life depended upon it—red rubber Crocodile pouch of Hignett's Cavalier, box of Bryant and May's matches, pipe, talismanic letters. He shrieked at himself in his head as he freed other cartridges of their clips and dropped them in his pocket. Mother, mother!

His life depended on a pocket full of cartridges. But supposing a cartridge still would not feed in? *Father was right. They should have been given a chance to fire their rifles.* He pulled back the bolt, and at once saw that the spring of the magazine was not strong enough to push the cartridge, already in position, into the chamber. The front stop clips were the wrong shape for pointed ammunition. The pointed end of the bullet would not feed in level; it tipped up, and when rammed in by the bolt, was sort of crushed. It was liable to explode like that, quite apart from the jamming.

Removing the magazine, he shook out the remaining cartridges, and put them in his pocket. Then slipping a round into the barrel, he closed the bolt, and fired it into the air. The butt in recoil struck his cheekbone, for he had been holding the rifle loosely: but the blow was not felt in the wild and trembling frenzy now that he had found out how to load. He looked from left to right, saw the long lines of men as far as the trees, and then with a secondary ice-shock realized that nothing could now save him from what was to happen when he reached the crackle of the skyline.

from *How Dear Is Life* by Henry Williamson

Canadians "going over the top", October 1916

The Last Laugh

"O Jesus Christ! I'm hit," he said; and died.
Whether he vainly cursed, or prayed indeed,
The Bullets chirped—In vain! vain! vain!
Machine-guns chuckled,—Tut-tut! Tut-tut!
And the Big Gun guffawed.

Another sighed,—"O Mother, mother! Dad!"
Then smiled, at nothing, childlike, being dead.
    And the lofty Shrapnel-cloud
    Leisurely gestured,—Fool!
    And the falling splinters tittered.

"My Love!" one moaned. Love-languid seemed his mood,
Till, slowly lowered, his whole face kissed the mud.
    And the Bayonets' long teeth grinned;
    Rabbles of Shells hooted and groaned;
    And the Gas hissed.

Wilfred Owen

From Albert to Bapaume

Lonely and bare and desolate,
Stretches of muddy filtered green,
A silence half articulate
Of all that those dumb eyes have seen.

A battered trench, a tree with boughs
Smutted and black with smoke and fire,
A solitary ruined house,
A crumpled mass of rusty wire.

And scarlet by each ragged fen
Long scattered ranks of poppies lay,
As though the blood of the dead men
Had not been wholly washed away.

Alec Waugh

Now it so happened that an infantry battalion had come down from
the lines to rest, and was quartered in the village. One of the ser-
geants had a case of rifle grenades. These were small bombs with a
long stalk which slipped down into the rifle barrel. You fired the
rifle and the bullet forced the stalk, with the bomb on the end of it,
out of the barrel, and theoretically it burst on hitting the enemy
trenches. His remarks about them were very much to the point:

"These 'ere bloody bombs are no bloody good! Either they
bloody well burst before you can shoot them off, or they don't
bloody well burst at all!" And he added further technical information about burst rifle barrels and wounded men.

This was an opportunity after Bodie's heart. He swapped a pair
of flying-gloves (which the sergeant thought might keep him warm
in the front line) for the case of rifle grenades and had it brought
down to the hangar, where its explosive possibilities made it much
respected by all the air mechanics! Not so by Bodie. A case of
bombs which could be induced to go off had the sort of lure a mouse-

trap must have to one of those experienced mice who know how it works! He proceeded to cast about for a method of utilizing this consignment of bombs for the discomfiture of the enemy.

Having hit on a plan, he sent for the carpenters and riggers and instructed them to make two small racks of three-ply wood with five holes in each, just large enough to hold the body of the grenade. In the Morane Parasol the observer's seat was immediately behind the pilot, and just behind and below it again was a small cupboard which held the wireless set. The two bomb racks were screwed on to the outside of the fuselage, one on either side, level with the wireless. The stalks of the grenades were unscrewed and replaced by pieces of tape which, by a complicated system of pulleys and guides, were led through and attached to a hook in the pilot's seat. Unfasten them, and the weight of the grenades would pull away the tapes and they would fall. Simple! But the rifle grenade was quite harmless until the fuse-pin in the head was removed, after which nothing could stop it going off in about three seconds. So Bodie devised a further system of pieces of string to withdraw the pins. In the cockpit, when all was complete, there were therefore ten pieces of string to release the fuses, and ten pieces of tape to release the grenades.

This piece of super-gadgetry completed, Bodie could hardly contain himself for delight. He invited every one to inspect the ingenuity of his contrivance, and decided to sally forth that very afternoon and drop these ten grenades on the Kaiser himself (for there was a rumour he was up at the line). Failing the All Highest, he was going to "bloody well drop them on the first thing he saw", and when a machine came back and reported Hun reinforcements moving out of Bapaume, some ten miles behind the lines, nothing could restrain him from departing immediately to blow them up.

"You see," he remarked naïvely, "they will never expect me to drop anything on them."

His accomplice in this dastardly scheme was a certain good-looking youth with wavy hair and a beautiful moustache. He was an observer and, strangely enough, did not seem very much concerned at the idea of flying over Germany with this Heath Robinson paraphernalia.

The machine was wheeled out, the grenades placed in position, the tapes adjusted, and at last all was ready. As they were about to leave, Bodie nearly upset the whole expedition by catching his foot in the gear as he climbed into the cockpit.

"Look out! Look out!" yelled a mechanic. "He's gone and pulled the pins out!"

Bodie remained suspended, with one leg in the air, like an ecstatic puppy at his first lamp-post, saying in rather a quavering voice, "It's all right, it's all right!"

When three seconds had elapsed and the aeroplane had not turned into a sort of Brock's benefit, they swung up the engine and were heartily glad to see the machine disappear "This side up with care" in the distance.

It was a beautiful evening, and nearly all of us were sitting about on some baulks of timber near the sheds smoking, talking, and waiting for the last of the afternoon patrol to return. At last, in the distance, a machine was seen staggering in a sort of drunken roll towards the aerodrome.

"Christ Almighty!" said the men who first saw it. "What the hell's happened to her?" As the machine came nearer it was seen that the fabric on one side of the fuselage had been ripped off and was flapping wildly in the wind. Needless to say, it was Bodie returning from his gallant attempt to Win the War.

When he landed there was a general stampede to the machine. The first thing noticeable was the good-looking face of the observer, who had, in this incredibly short space of time, grown a beard, consisting of small pieces of red vulcanite which were sticking into all parts of his chin and cheeks. He climbed out of the machine, using the sort of language which will remain for ever unprintable, and a cheer went up when it was seen that his posterior had been the recipient of the disintegrated components of the wireless set! Condensers and transformers, one end well embedded in his anatomy, waved jovially in the air. His breeches were torn, his coat in ribbons. He was badly shaken, trembling and laughing.

"What happened? What happened?" And, when the first convulsions of merriment had died down:

"One of those bloody bombs," he said, cautiously rubbing his backside, "went off."

So much was obvious. The fuselage was a wreck. One of the longerons had been blown right through. Two or three struts and a dozen wires had been snapped. By a miracle the controls had remained intact. Bodie climbed out of the machine. He surveyed the wreckage with an expression of pained surprise.

"It's a pity about that," he remarked. And then he told the story. He had flown over to Bapaume and failed to find the enemy reinforcements. However, he spotted a number of Huns in a trench and came down to do his deadly work.

"I'm going to drop them," he shouted. "Look out!" And the observer did!

Bodie withdrew the strings, converting ten harmless grenades into ten extremely dangerous ones, and a second later released the tapes. They all fell clear (incidentally doing no damage whatever where they fell) except one, which got caught, and hung there dangling on its tape. A second later it burst.

It was two days before the machine was serviceable again. In the interval Bodie was busy planning a more complicated apparatus to drop double the quantity of grenades. But one of the Flight-Sergeants, either on receipt of instructions or else from motives of self-preservation (he might have had to go up with Bodie himself), privily took the case of grenades out of the sheds one night and had it dropped in the river near by.

Bodie never quite got over its disappearance, and used to wander about muttering vague imprecations about sabotage in the Royal Flying Corps.

from Sagittarius Rising by Cecil Lewis

I can never express in writing what I feel about the men in the trenches; and nobody who has not seen them can ever understand. According to the present routine, we stay in the front line eight days and nights; then go out for the same period. Each company spends four days and four nights in the fire-trench before being relieved. The men are practically without rest. They are wet through most of the time. They are shelled and trench-mortared. They may not be hit, but they are kept in a perpetual state of unrest and strain.

They work all night and every night, and a good part of each day, digging and filling sandbags, and repairing the breaches in the breastworks; that is, when they are not on sentry. The temperature is icy. They have not even a blanket. The last two days it has been snowing. They cannot move more than a few feet from their posts; therefore, except when they are actually digging, they cannot keep themselves warm by exercise; and, when they try to sleep, they freeze. At present, they are getting a tablespoon of rum to console them, once in three days.

Think of these things, and compare them with what are considered serious hardships in normal life! Yet these men play their part uncomplainingly. That is to say, they never complain seriously. Freezing, or snowing, or drenching rain; always smothered with mud; you may ask any one of them, any moment of the day or night, "Are you cold?" or "Are you wet?"—and you will get but one answer. The Irishman will reply—always with a smile—"Not too cold, sir," or "Not too wet, sir." It makes me feel sick.

It makes me think I never want to see the British Isles again so long as the war lasts. It makes one feel ashamed for those Irishmen, and also of those fellow-countrymen of our own, earning huge wages, yet for ever clamouring for more; striking, or threatening to strike; while the country is engaged upon this murderous struggle. Why, we ask here, has not the whole nation, civil as well as military, been conscripted?

The curious thing is that all seem so much more contented here than the people at home. The poor Tommy, shivering in the trenches, is happier than the beast who makes capital out of the war. Everybody laughs at everything, here. It is the only way. . . .

from War Letters to a Wife by Lt.-Col. Rowland Feilding

"Well, if you knows of a better 'ole, go to it."

Fellow citizens, Conscription is now law in this country and our free traditions and our hard-won liberties have been violated. Conscription means the desecration of principles that we have long held dear. It involves the subordination of civil liberties. Military dictation imperils the freedom of individual conscience and establishes in our midst that militarism which menaces all social progress and divides the peoples of all nations. We reaffirm our determined resistance to all that is established by the Act. We cannot assist in warfare. War, which to us is wrong, war which the peoples do not seek, can only be made impossible when men who so believe, remain steadfast to their convictions. Conscience, it is true, has been recognized in the Act, but it has been placed at the mercy of tribunals. We are pre-

45

pared to answer for our faith before any tribunal, but we cannot accept any exemption that would compel those who hate war to kill by proxy, or to set them to tasks which would help to further the War. We strongly condemn the monstrous assumption by Parliament that a man is deemed to be bound by an oath that he has never taken and forced under an authority he will never acknowledge to perform acts which outrage his deepest convictions. It is true that the passing of the Act applies only to a small section of the community, but a great tradition has been sacrificed. Already there is clamour for the extension of the Act. Admit the principle and who can stay the march of militarism ? Repeal the Act—that is your only safeguard. If this be not done militarism will fasten its iron grip on our national life and institutions, and there will be imposed upon us the very system which our statesmen affirm they set out to dethrone. What shall it profit a nation if it shall win the War but lose its own soul ?—Signed on behalf of the No-conscription Fellowship.

Quoted in House of Commons—from *Hansard*, June 1st 1916

The Happy Warrior

His wild heart beats with painful sobs,
His strain'd hands clench an ice-cold rifle,
His aching jaws grip a hot parch'd tongue,
His wide eyes search unconsciously.

He cannot shriek.

Bloody saliva
Dribbles down his shapeless jacket.

I saw him stab
And stab again
A well-killed Boche.

This is the happy warrior,
This is he . . .

Herbert Read

My dear Catherine: I never wrote to tell you that they gave me a complete exemption from all military service, thanks be to God. That was a week ago last Thursday. I had to join the Colours in Penzance, be conveyed to Bodmin (60 miles), spend a night in barracks with all the other men, and then be examined. It was experience enough for me, of soldiering. I am sure I should die in a week, if they kept me. It is the annulling of all one stands for, this militarism, the nipping of the very germ of one's being. I was very much upset. The sense of spiritual disaster everywhere was quite terrifying. One was not sure whether one survived or not. Things are very bad.

Yet I liked the men. They all seemed so *decent*. And yet they all seemed as if they had *chosen wrong*. It was the underlying sense of disaster that overwhelmed me. They are all so brave, to suffer, but none of them brave enough, to reject suffering. They are all so noble, to accept sorrow and hurt, but they can none of them demand happiness. Their manliness all lies in accepting calmly this death, this loss of their integrity. They must stand by their fellow man: that is the motto. . . . This is what the love of our neighbour has brought us to, that, because one man dies, we all die.

This is the most terrible madness. And the worst of it all, is, that it is a madness of righteousness. . . . There is no falsity about it: they believe in their duty to their fellow man. And what duty is this, which makes us forfeit everything, because Germany invaded Belgium? Is there nothing beyond my fellow man? If not, then there is nothing beyond myself, beyond my own throat, which may be cut, and my own purse, which may be slit: because *I* am the fellow-man of all the world, my neighbour is but myself in a mirror. So we toil in a circle of pure egoism. . . .

There needs something else besides the love of the neighbour. If all my neighbours chose to go down the slope to Hell, that is no reason why I should go with them. I know in my own soul a truth, a right, and no amount of neighbours can weight it out of the balance. I know that, for me, the war is wrong. I know that if the Germans wanted my little house, I would rather give it them than fight for it: because my little house is not important enough to me.

If another man must fight for his house, the more's the pity. But it is his affair. To fight for possessions, goods, is what my soul *will not* do. Therefore it will not fight for the neighbour who fights for his own goods.

All this war, this talk of nationality, to me is false. I *feel* no nationality, not fundamentally. I feel no passion for my own land, nor my own house, nor my own furniture, nor my own money. Therefore I won't pretend any. Neither will I take part in the scrimmage, to help my neighbour. It is his affair to go in or to stay out, as he wishes. . . .

from D. H. Lawrence's letter to Catherine Carswell, July 9th 1916

Returning, We Hear the Larks

Sombre the night is.
And though we have our lives, we know
What sinister threat lurks there.

Dragging these anguished limbs, we only know
This poison-blasted track opens on our camp—
On a little safe sleep.

But hark! joy—joy—strange joy.
Lo! heights of night ringing with unseen larks.
Music showering on our upturned list'ning faces.

Death could drop from the dark
As easily as song—
But song only dropped,
Like a blind man's dreams on the sand
By dangerous tides,
Like a girl's dark hair for she dreams no ruin lies there,
Or her kisses where a serpent hides.

Isaac Rosenberg

Dulce Et Decorum Est

Bent double, like old beggars under sacks,
Knock-kneed, coughing like hags, we cursed through sludge,
Till on the haunting flares we turned our backs,
And towards our distant rest began to trudge.
Men marched asleep. Many had lost their boots
But limped on, blood-shod. All went lame; all blind;
Drunk with fatigue; deaf even to the hoots
Of gas-shells dropping softly behind.

Gas! GAS! Quick, boys!—An ecstasy of fumbling,
Fitting the clumsy helmets just in time;
But someone still was yelling out and stumbling
And floundering like a man in fire or lime . . .
Dim through the misty panes and thick green light,
As under a green sea, I saw him drowning.

In all my dreams, before my helpless sight,
He plunges at me, guttering, choking, drowning.

If in some smothering dreams you too could pace
Behind the wagon that we flung him in,
And watch the white eyes writhing in his face,
His hanging face, like a devil's sick of sin;
If you could hear, at every jolt, the blood
Come gargling from the froth-corrupted lungs,
Obscene as cancer, bitter as the cud
Of vile, incurable sores on innocent tongues,—
My friend, you would not tell with such high zest
To children ardent for some desperate glory,
The old Lie: Dulce et decorum est
Pro patria mori.

Wilfred Owen

Does It Matter?

Does it matter?—losing your legs?...
For people will always be kind,
And you need not show that you mind
When the others come in after hunting
To gobble their muffins and eggs.

Does it matter?—losing your sight?...
There's such splendid work for the blind;
And people will always be kind,
As you sit on the terrace remembering
And turning your face to the light.

Do they matter?—those dreams from the pit?...
You can drink and forget and be glad,
And people won't say that you're mad;
For they'll know you've fought for your country
And no one will worry a bit.

Siegfried Sassoon

When at last Mr. Rhys left them, they relaxed into ease with a sigh. Major Shadwell and Captain Malet they could understand, because each was what every private soldier is, a man in arms against a world, a man fighting desperately for himself, and conscious that, in the last resort, he stood alone; for such self-reliance lies at the very heart of comradeship. In so far as Mr. Rhys had something of the same character, they respected him; but when he spoke to them of patriotism, sacrifice, and duty, he merely clouded and confused their vision.

"Chaps," said Weeper, suddenly, "for Christ's sake let's pray for rain!"

"What good would that do?" said Pacey, reasonably. "If they don't send us over the top here, they'll send us over somewhere else. It 'as got to be, an' if it 'as got to be, the sooner it's over an' done wi' the better. If we die, we die, an' it won't trouble nobody, leastways not for long it won't; an' if we don't die now, we'd 'ave to die some other time."

"What d'you want to talk about dyin' for?" said Martlow, resentfully. "I'd rather kill some other mucker first. I want to have my fling before I die, I do."

"If you want to pray, you 'ad better pray for the war to stop," continued Pacey, "so as we can all go back to our own 'omes in peace. I'm a married man wi' two children, an' I don't say I'm any better'n the next man, but I've a bit o' religion in me still, an' I don't hold wi' sayin' such things in jest."

"Aye," said Madeley, bitterly; "an' what good will all your

51

prayin' do you? If there were any truth in religion, would there be a war, would God let it go on?"

"Some on us blame God for our own faults," said Pacey, coolly, "an' it were men what made the war. It's no manner o' use us sittin' 'ere pityin' ourselves, an' blaming God for our own faults. I've got nowt to say again Mr. Rhys. 'E talks about liberty, an' fightin' for your country, an' posterity, an' so on; but what I want to know is what all us 'ns are fightin' for. . . ."

"We're fightin' for all we've bloody got," said Madeley, bluntly.

"An' that's sweet FA," said Weeper Smart. "A tell thee, that all a want to do is to save me own bloody skin. An' the first thing a do, when a go into t' line, is to find out where t' bloody dressing-stations are; an' if a can get a nice blighty, chaps, when once me face is turned towards home, I'm laughing. You won't see me bloody arse for dust. A'm not proud. A tell thee straight. Them as thinks different can 'ave all the bloody war they want, and me own share of it, too."

"Well, what the 'ell did you come out for?" asked Madeley.

Weeper lifted up a large, spade-like hand with the solemnity of one making an affirmation.

"That's where th'ast got me beat, lad," he admitted. "When a saw all them as didn' know any better'n we did joinin' up, an' a went walkin' out wi' me girl on Sundays, as usual, a just felt ashamed. An' a put it away, an' a put it away, until in th' end it got me down. I knew what it'd be, but it got the better o' me, an' then, like a bloody fool, a went an' joined up too. A were ashamed to be seen walkin' in the streets, a were. But a tell thee, now, that if a were once out o' these togs an' in civvies again, a wouldn't mind all the shame in the world; no, not if I 'ad to slink through all the back streets, an' didn't dare put my nose in t'Old Vaults again. A've no pride left in me now, chaps, an' that's the plain truth a'm tellin'. Let them as made the war come an' fight it, that's what a say."

"That's what I say, too," said Glazier, a man of about Madeley's age, with an air of challenge. Short, stocky, and ruddy like Madeley, he was of coarser grain, with an air of brutality that the other lacked: the kind of man who, when he comes to grips, kills, and grunts with pleasure in killing. "Why should us'ns fight an' be killed for all them bloody slackers at 'ome? It ain't right. No matter

52

what they say, it ain't right. We're doin' our duty, an' they ain't, an' they're coinin' money while we get ten bloody frong a week. They don't care a blow about us. Once we're in the army, they've got us by the short 'airs. Talk about discipline! They don't try disciplinin' any o' them muckin' civvies, do they? We want to put some o' them bloody politicians in the front line, an' see 'em shelled to shit. That'd buck their ideas up."

"I'm not fightin' for a lot o' bloody civvies," said Madeley, reasonably. "I'm fightin' for myself an' me own folk. It's all bloody fine sayin' let them as made the war fight it. 'Twere Germany made the war."

"A tell thee," said Weeper, positively, "there are thousands o' poor beggars, over there in the German lines, as don' know, no more'n we do ourselves, what it's all about."

"Then what do the silly muckers come an' fight for?" asked Madeley, indignantly. "Why didn't they stay 't 'ome? Tha'lt be sayin' next that the Frenchies sent 'em an invite."

"What a say is, that it weren't none o' our business. We'd no call to mix ourselves up wi' other folks' quarrels," replied Weeper.

"Well, I don't hold wi' that," said Glazier, judicially. "I'm not fightin' for them bloody slackers an' conchies at 'ome; but what I say is that the Fritzes 'ad to be stopped. If we 'adn't come in, an' they'd got the Frenchies beat, 'twould 'a' been our turn next."

"Too bloody true it would," said Madeley, "An' I'd rather come an' fight Fritz in France than 'ave 'im come over to Blighty an' start bashin' our 'ouses about, same as 'e's done 'ere."

" 'E'd never 'ave come to England. The Navy 'd 'ave seen to that," said Pacey.

"Don't you be too bloody sure about the Navy," said Corporal Hamley, entering into the discussion at last. "The Navy 'as got all it can bloody well do, as things are."

"Well, chaps," said Glazier, "maybe I'm right an' maybe I'm wrong, but that's neither here nor there; only I've sometimes thought it would be a bloody good thing for us'ns, if the 'un did land a few troops in England. Show 'em what war's like. Madeley an' I struck it lucky an' went 'ome on leaf together, an' you never seed anythink like it. Windy! Like a lot o' bloody kids they was, an' talking no more sense; 'pon me word, you'd be surprised at some o' the questions they'd ask, an' you couldn't answer sensible. They'd never believe it, if you did. We jes' kep' our mouths shut, and told 'em the war was all right, and we'd got it won, but not yet. 'Twas the only way to keep 'em quiet.

"The boozers in Wes'church was shut most of the day; but Madeley and I would go down to the Greyhound, at seven o'clock, an' it was always chock-a-block wi' chaps lappin' it up as fast as they could, before closin' time. There'd be some old sweats, and some men back from the 'ospital into barracks, but not fit, an' a few new recruits; but most o' them were miners, the sort o' bleeders who took our job to dodge gettin' into khaki. Bloody fine miners they was. Well, one Saturday night we was in there 'avin' a bit of a booze-up, but peaceable like, when one of them bloody miners came in an' asked us to 'ave a drink in a loud voice. Well, we were peaceable enough, an' I dare say we might 'ave 'ad a drink with 'im, but the swine put 'is fist into 'is trousers' pocket, and pulls out a fistful of Bradburys an' 'arf-crowns, an' plunks 'em down on the bar counter. 'There,' he says, 'there's me bloody wages for a week, an' I ain't done more'n eight hours' work for it, either. I don't care if the bloody war lasts for ever,' 'e says. I looks up an' sees Madeley lookin' white an' dangerous. 'Was you talkin' to me?' says Madeley. 'Aye,' 'e says. 'Well, take that, you muckin' bastard!' says Madeley, an' sloshes 'im one in the clock. Some of 'is friends interfered first, and then some of our friends interfered, an' in five seconds there was 'ell's delight in the bloody bar, wi' the old bitch be'ind the counter goin' into 'ysterics, an' 'ollerin' for the police.

"Then Madeley got 'old of 'is man, who was blubberin' an' swearin' summat awful, an' near twisted 'is arm off. I were busy keepin' some o' the other muckers off 'im, but 'e didn't pay no attention to nobody else, 'e just lugged 'is man out the back door an' into the yard, wi' the old girl 'ollerin' blue murder; and Madeley lugs 'im into the urinal, an' gets 'im down an' rubs 'is face in it. I'd got out the back door too, be that time, as I seed some red-caps comin' into the bar; an' when 'e'd finished I saw Madeley stand up an' wipe 'is 'ands on the seat of 'is trousers. 'There, you bastard,' 'e says; 'now you go 'ome an' talk to yourself.'—' 'Op it,' I says to 'im, 'there's the bloody picket outside'; an' we 'opped it over some palin's at the bottom o' the yard; and one of 'em came away, an' I run a bloody great splinter into the palm o' me 'and. Then we just beggared off, by some back streets, to The Crown, an' 'ad a couple o' pints an' went 'ome peaceable."

"Look at ol' tear-gas!" Martlow cried. 'Thought you didn't like fightin', Weeper?"

Weeper's whole face was alight with excitement.

"A like a scrap as well as any man, so long as it don't go too far," said Weeper. "A'd 'ave given a lot to see thee go for that miner, Madeley. It's them chaps what are always on the make, an' don't care 'ow they makes it, as causes 'arf the wars. Them's the bloody cowards."

"Is it all true, Madeley?" asked Corporal Hamley.

"It were summat like, but I misremember," said Madeley, modestly. "But it's all true what 'e says about folks at 'ome, most on 'em. They don't care a rap what 'appens to us'ns, so long as they can keep a 'ole skin. Say they be ready to make any sacrifice; but we're the bloody sacrifice. You never seed such a windy lot; an' bloodthirsty ain't the word for it. They've all gone potty. You'd think your best friends wouldn't be satisfied till they'd seed your name on the roll of honour. I tol' one of 'em 'e knew a bloody sight more'n I did about the war. The only person as 'ad any sense was me mother. She on'y fussed about what I wanted to eat. She didn't want to know anything about the war, an' it were on'y me she were afraid for. She didn't min' about aught else. 'Please God, you'll be home soon,' she'd say. An' please God I will."

"An' then they give you a bloody party," said Glazier. "Madeley an' I went to one. You should a seed some o' the pushers. Girls o' seventeen painted worse nor any Gerties I'd ever knowed. One of 'em came on an' sang a lot o' songs wi' dirty meanings to 'em. I remember one she sang wi' another girl, *I want a Rag*. She did an' all, too. When this bloody war's over, you'll go back to England an' fin' nought there but a lot o' conchies and bloody prostitutes."

"There's good an' bad," said Pacey, mildly, "an' if there's more bad than good, I don't know but the good don't wear better. But there's nought sure in this world, no more."

"No, an' never 'as been," said Madeley, pessimistically.

"There's nought sure for us'ns, anyway," said Weeper, relapsing. "Didst 'ear what Cap'n Thompson read out this mornin', about stoppin' to 'elp any poor beggar what was wounded? The bloody brass-'at what wrote that letter 'as never been in any big show 'isself, that a dare swear. 'E's one o' them muckers as is never nearer to the real thing than GHQ."

"You don't want to talk like that," said Corporal Hamley. "You've 'ad your orders."

"A don't mind tellin' thee, corporal," said Weeper, again lifting a large flat hand, as though by that gesture he stopped the mouths of all the world. "A don't mind tellin' thee, that if a see a chum o' mine down, an' a can do aught to 'elp 'im, all the brass 'ats in the British Army, an' there's a bloody sight too many o' 'em, aren't goin' to stop me. A'll do what's right, an' if a know aught about thee, tha'lt do as a do."

"You don't want to talk about it, anyway," said Corporal Hamley, quietly. "I'm not sayin' you're not right: I'd do what any other man'd do; but there's no need to make a song about it."

"What beats me," said Shem, sniggering, "is that the bloody fool who wrote that instructional letter doesn't seem to know what any ordinary man would do in the circumstances. We all know that there must be losses, you can't expect to take a trench without some casualties; but they seem to go on from saying that losses are unavoidable, to thinking that they're necessary, and from that, to thinking that they don't matter."

"They don't know what we've got to go through, that's the truth of it," said Weeper. "They measure the distance, an' they count the men, an' the guns, an' think a battle's no' but a sum you can do wi' a pencil an' a bit o' paper.

"I heard Mr. Pardew talking to Mr. Rhys about a course he'd been on, and he told him a brass-hat had been lecturing them on the lessons of the Somme offensive, and gave them an estimate of the total German losses; and then an officer at the back of the room got up, and asked him, if he could give them any information about the British losses, and the brass-hat said: No, and looked at them as though they were a lot of criminals."

"It's a fact," said Glazier; "whether you're talkin' to a civvy or whether you're talkin' to a brass 'at, an' some o' the officers aren't no better, if you tell the truth, they think you're a bloody coward. They've not got our experience, an' they don't face it as us'ns do."

56

"Give them a chance," said Bourne, reasonably; he hadn't spoken before, he usually sat back and listened quietly to these debates.

"Let 'em take my bloody chance!" shouted Weeper, vindictively.

"There's a good deal in what you say," said Bourne, who was a little embarrassed by the way they all looked at him suddenly. "I think there's a good deal of truth in it; but after all, what is a brass-hat's job? He's not thinking of you or of me or of any individual man, or of any particular battalion or division. Men, to him, are only part of the material he has got to work with; and if he felt as you or I feel, he couldn't carry on with his job. It's not fair to think he's inhuman. He's got to draw up a plan, from rather scrappy information, and it is issued in the form of an order; but he knows very well something may happen at any moment to throw everything out of gear. The original plan is no more than a kind of map; you can't see the country by looking at a map, and you can't see the fighting by looking at a plan of attack. Once we go over the top it's the colonel's and the company commander's job. Once we meet a Hun it's our job. . . ."

"Yes, an' our job's a bloody sight worse'n theirs," said Weeper.

"It's not worse than the colonel's or the company commander's," said Bourne. "Anyway, they come over with us. They've got to lead us, or drive us. They may have to order us to do something, knowing damned well that they're spending us. I don't envy them. I think that bit in the letter, about not stopping to help the wounded, is silly. It's up to us, that is; but it's up to us not to make another man's agony our excuse. What's bloody silly in the letter is the last bit, where they say they don't anticipate any serious resistance from the enemy. That is the Staff's job, and they ought to know it better."

"We started talking about what we were fighting for," said Shem laughing. "It was Mr. Rhys started it."

"Yes, an' you've been talkin' all over the bloody shop ever since," said Corporal Hamley. "You all ought to be on the bloody staff, you ought. 'Oo are orderly-men? Shem and Martlow; well, tea's up."

Shem and Martlow looked at the straight rain, and then struggled into their greatcoats.

"All that a says is, if a man's dead it don't matter no more to 'im 'oo wins the bloody war," said Weeper. "We're 'ere, there's no gettin' away from that, corporal, 'ere we are, an' since we're 'ere, we're just fightin' for ourselves; we're just fightin' for ourselves, an' for each other."

from Her Privates We by Frederic Manning

Because We're Here

We're here because we're here because
We're here because we're here:
We're here because we're here because
We're here because we're here.

Sung to the tune of Auld Lang Syne

It was during the later part of 1917 that the food shortage became more and more serious, and in consequence control more strict. To throw rice at a wedding became a summary offence and the sale of luxury chocolates was stopped. No sweetmeats over 2d. per oz. or chocolates over 3d. per oz. were permitted, the use of starch in laundry work was restricted, horses and cows and even the London pigeons were rationed, no corn was allowed for cobs, hunters, carriage horses and hacks, most of which had by then been commandeered for Army use.

A man was fined £50 for collecting bread crusts for pig food, and in defence said that otherwise they would have been wasted, as navvies would not eat crusts. The amount of bread or cake which might be sold at tea shops for afternoon tea was reduced to 2 oz.

It became an offence to adopt and feed stray dogs; these innocent victims of war had to be handed over to the police. Local food controllers were appointed, butchers were ordered to display price lists, and bakers were forbidden to bake any but Government regulation bread. This bread was compounded from various ingredients, including barley, rice, maize, beans, oatmeal, and in

October 1917 bakers were permitted to add potato in the proportion of 1 lb. to 7 lb. of flour. . . .

When November came there was a great to-do about the Lord Mayor's banquet. It was thought that it should not take place, but the Lord Mayor did not agree. The guests were allowed petrol in order to drive to it, and the table appointments included menu cards 12 by 18 inches. And at this time we were publicly advised "Eat slowly: you will need less food. Keep warm: you will need less food." How we were to keep warm when fuel was strictly rationed and we were chilly as the result of an insufficiently fat diet was not explained.

As Christmas drew near the Ministry of Food planned a patriotic Christmas dinner for us, which consisted of French rice soup, filleted haddock, roast fowl and vegetables, plum pudding, caramel custard. This, it was said, would cost 10s. 2d. for four people. . . .

By that time we were in receipt of sugar tickets. Milk was the first item of our dietary to be controlled, and sugar the first for which ration cards were issued. Hundreds of girls under eighteen were employed at £1 per week on sugar-card registration work. It was notified that their education was to be continued to fit them for other employment.

By now so great were the discomfort and ill-feeling caused by the food queues, and the suspicion that the rich were obtaining more than their fair share of eatables, that the demand for compulsory rations became more and more insistent. Anyone who penetrated the poorer neighbourhoods became familiar with the queue. In the bitter cold and rain of that depressing winter of 1917 women and children waited outside the shabby shops common to the poor districts of all towns.

They carried baskets, string bags, fish basses, bags made of American cloth, and babies, and stood, shifting their burdens from one arm to another to ease their aching. Often, in spite of cold, rain and weariness, there was a flow of wit. Sometimes a late comer would try to sneak in at the head of the line, and then there would be trouble, promptly allayed by the policeman or Special Constable, or in some provincial towns the policewoman.

The middle classes, who could not obtain servants or whose servants had other work to do than go out shopping, also swelled the queues. . . . Women used to go from shop to shop trying to find one at which they could buy meat or margarine, tea, and possibly a little extra sugar.

The rich escaped these unpleasant tasks, partly because they could send servants to shop for them and partly because the customer who bought on a large scale could still have his goods delivered at his house, though by now the cart or motor was generally in charge of a woman, and women had taken the place of the younger men both in butchers' and grocers' shops.

Notices were displayed in shops and stores asking customers to carry their own parcels whenever possible, and roomy baskets and bags became fashionable adjuncts to the toilette. The master bakers begged customers not to waste the time of their employees by chatting to them when they delivered goods. The conduct of certain trades-people who at this time shut their shops to the general public and sent out meat and other goods to favoured customers via the back door infuriated the people, and occasionally luckless butcher boys were held up and the contents of their baskets looted. The knowledge that some well-to-do folk were hoarding food also caused discontent. It was these annoyances which made local authorities adopt rationing schemes before national compulsory rationing came into force. One of the first cities to do so was Birmingham.

One sympathizes with a housewife who had two sons fighting, whose cook fell ill of that terrible influenza which attacked us in 1917 and 1918, whose house-parlourmaid was so frightened by air raids that she ran away back to her home in the country, and who was left to do the house work, to buy food—very little of which could then be delivered owing to shortage of transport, and much of which had to be waited for in a queue—nurse the invalid and cook for the cook, herself and an overworked Government official husband. . . .

After February 1918 veal was no longer on sale, and it became impossible in London and the six home counties to buy butter, margarine or meat without cards. The allowance generally procurable was 1½ lb. of meat per head per week for adults, for children under ten 10 oz., butter or margarine 4 oz., and sugar 8 oz. Travellers' ration cards were issued, and those children who went to boarding-schools had to take their ration cards with them. Along with notices about school clothes, possible infection and times of trains came the demand, "Please do not forget ration cards." A girl who was then a child at school recalls the sight of rows of little jam pots, each labelled with its owner's name, arranged on shelves in the dining-room. These contained the ration of margarine. If any were left it was used to make pastry for a Sunday and rather sugarless tart. . . .

By then the supply of servants was even shorter than the supply of food. In a letter from a boy at a public school he mentions that all the waiters have been called up and that boys take it in turn to wait at table, and that they make their own beds. The posts of the younger masters who became soldiers were filled by elderly retired teachers. The boys bitterly regretted their youth and their inability to take part in the war.

By the end of April 1918 the national rationing of meat came into force, and everyone was required to register for bacon also. Owing to the scarcity of meat, fancy prices for offal and poultry were charged, and in some places the butchers' shops opened only for about one hour a day. The rations of the Home Army were reduced, and it became legal to inflict a fine up to £400 for hoarding. . . .

Our difficulties and discomforts were added to by the prevalence of influenza, which in many cases developed into pneumonia. It was difficult to obtain nurses or drugs or sufficient nourishing food for invalids. In one house—by no means an unusual case—but one person out of a family of three and three servants was able to get about. Charwomen were not to be had, and a man friend, on his return from his Ministry, used to carry coals and help wash up. . . .

By the end of July the public knew that all fear of starvation owing to the German blockade was ended, but that supplies must continue to be limited and prices remain high. Considering the suffering and discomfort due to these causes, to the shortage of fuel, overwork, personal unhappiness and general mental strain, the people as a whole remained wonderfully calm. They grumbled, but their grumbling was chiefly an emotional outlet. Directly they understood the position, though they might still grumble, there remained the determination to "stick it", to do their "bit" and to win the war.

from How We Lived Then by Mrs C. S. Peel

Judas and the Profiteer

Judas descended to this lower Hell
    To meet his only friend—the profiteer—
Who, looking fat and rubicund and well,
    Regarded him, and then said with a sneer,
"Iscariot, they did you! Fool! to sell
For silver pence the body of God's Son,
Whereas from maiming men with tank and shell
    I gain at least a golden million."

But Judas answered: "You deserve your gold;
It's not His body but His soul *you've* sold!"

Osbert Sitwell

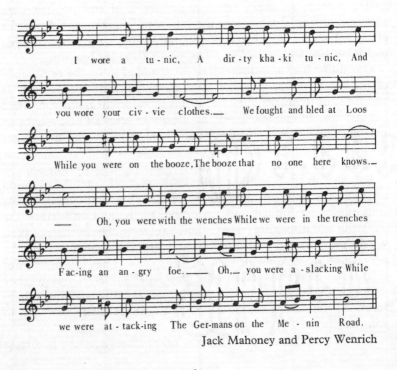

I wore a tunic, A dirty khaki tunic, And
you wore your civvie clothes. We fought and bled at Loos
While you were on the booze, The booze that no one here knows.
Oh, you were with the wenches While we were in the trenches
Facing an angry foe. Oh, you were a-slacking While
we were attacking The Germans on the Menin Road.

Jack Mahoney and Percy Wenrich

It is pleasant to sit quietly somewhere, in the beer garden for example, under the chestnuts by the skittle-alley. The leaves fall down on the table and on the ground, only a few, the first. A glass of beer stands in front of me. I've learned to drink in the army. The glass is half empty, but there are a few good swigs ahead of me, and besides I can always order a second and a third if I wish to. There are no bugles and no bombardments, the children of the house play in the skittle-alley, and the dog rests his head against my knee. The sky is blue, between the leaves of the chestnut rises the green spire of St. Margaret's Church.

This is good, I like it. But I cannot get on with the people. My mother is the only one who asks no questions. Not so my father. He wants me to tell him about the front; he is curious in a way that I find stupid and distressing; I no longer have any real contact with him. There is nothing he likes more than just hearing about it. I realize he does not know that a man cannot talk of such things; I would do it willingly, but it is too dangerous for me to put these things into words. I am afraid they might then become gigantic and I be no longer able to master them. What would become of us if everything that happens out there were quite clear to us?

So I confine myself to telling him a few amusing things. But he wants to know whether I have ever had a hand-to-hand fight. I say "No," and get up and go out.

But that does not mend matters. After I have been startled a couple of times in the street by the screaming of the tramcars, which resembles the shriek of a shell coming straight for one, somebody taps me on the shoulder. It is my German-master, and he fastens on me with the usual question: "Well, how are things out there? Terrible, terrible, eh? Yes, it is dreadful, but we must carry on. And after all, you do at least get decent food out there, so I hear. You look well, Paul, and fit. Naturally it's worse here. Naturally. The best for our soldiers every time, that goes without saying."

He drags me along to a table with a lot of others. They welcome me, a headmaster shakes hands with me and says: "So you come from the front? What is the spirit like out there? Excellent, eh? excellent?"

I explain that no one would be sorry to be back home.

He laughs uproariously. "I can well believe it! But first you have to give the Froggies a good hiding. Do you smoke? Here, try one. Waiter, bring a beer as well for our young warrior."

Unfortunately I have accepted the cigar, so I have to remain. And they are all so dripping with good will that it is impossible to object. All the same I feel annoyed and smoke like a chimney as hard as I can. In order to make at least some show of appreciation I toss off the beer in one gulp. Immediately a second is ordered; people know how much they are indebted to the soldiers. They argue about what we ought to annex. The headmaster with the steel watch-chain wants to have at least the whole of Belgium, the coal-areas of France, and a slice of Russia. He produces reasons why we must have them and is quite inflexible until at last the others give in to him. Then he begins to expound just whereabouts in France the breakthrough must come, and turns to me: "Now, shove ahead a bit out there with your everlasting trench warfare—Smash through the Johnnies and then there will be peace."

I reply that in our opinion a breakthrough may not be possible. The enemy may have too many reserves. Besides, the war may be rather different from what people think.

He dismisses the idea loftily and informs me I know nothing about it. "The details, yes," says he, "but this relates to the whole. And of that you are not able to judge. You see only your little sector and so cannot have any general survey. You do your duty, you risk your lives, that deserves the highest honour—every man of you ought to have the Iron Cross—but first of all the enemy line must be broken through in Flanders and then rolled up from the top."

He blows his nose and wipes his beard. "Completely rolled up they must be, from the top to the bottom. And then to Paris."

I would like to know just how he pictures it to himself, and pour the third glass of beer into me. Immediately he orders another.

But I break away. He stuffs a few more cigars into my pocket and sends me off with a friendly slap. "All of the best! I hope we will soon hear something worthwhile from you."

*   *   *   *   *

I imagined leave would be different from this. Indeed, it was different a year ago. It is I of course that have changed in the interval. There lies a gulf between that time and today. At that time I still knew nothing about the war, we had only been in quiet sectors. But now I see that I have been crushed without knowing it. I find I do not belong here any more, it is a foreign world. Some of these people ask questions, some ask no questions, but one can see that the latter are proud of themselves for their silence; they often say with a wise air that these things cannot be talked about. They plume themselves on it.

I prefer to be alone, so that no one troubles me. For they all come back to the same thing, how badly it goes and how well it goes; one thinks it is this way, another that; and yet they are always absorbed in the things that go to make up their existence. Formerly I lived in just the same way myself, but now I feel no contact here.

They talk too much for me. They have worries, aims, desires, that I cannot comprehend. I often sit with one of them in the little beer garden and try to explain to him that this is really the only thing: just to sit quietly, like this. They understand of course, they agree, they may even feel it so too, but only with words, only with words, yes, that is it—they feel it, but always with only half of themselves, the rest of their being is taken up with other things, they are so divided in themselves that none feels it with his whole essence; I cannot even say myself exactly what I mean.

When I see them here, in their rooms, in their offices, about their occupations, I feel an irresistible attraction in it, I would like to be here too and forget the war; but also it repels me, it is so narrow, how can that fill a man's life, he ought to smash it to bits; how can they do it, while out at the front the splinters are whining over the shell-holes and the star-shells go up, the wounded are carried back on waterproof sheets and comrades crouch in the trenches.—They are different men here, men I cannot properly understand, whom I envy and despise.

from *All Quiet on the Western Front* by Erich Maria Remarque

A MOTHER'S ANSWER TO
"A COMMON SOLDIER."

SIR,— As a mother of an only child—a son now in training and waiting for the age limit to do his bit—may I be permitted to reply to Tommy Atkins, whose letter appeared in your issue of the 9th inst.? Perhaps he will kindly convey to his friends in the trenches, not what the Government thinks, not what the Pacifists think, but what the mothers of the British race think of our fighting men. It is a voice which demands to be heard, seeing that we play the most important part in the history of the world, for it is we who "mother the men" who have to uphold the honour and traditions not only of our Empire, but of the whole civilised world.

To the man who pathetically calls himself a "common soldier," may I say that we women, who demand to be heard, will tolerate no such cry as "Peace! Peace!" where there is no peace. The corn that will wave over land watered by the blood of our brave lads shall testify to the future that their blood was not spilt in vain. We need no marble monuments to remind us. We only need that force of character behind all motives to see this monstrous world tragedy brought to a victorious ending. The blood of the dead and the dying, the blood of the "common soldier" from his "slight wounds" will not cry out to us in vain. They have all done their share, and we, as women, will do ours without murmuring and without complaint. Send the Pacifists to us and we shall very soon show them, and show the world, that in our homes at least there shall be no "sitting at home warm and cosy in the winter, cool and 'comfy' in the summer." There is only one temperature for the women of the British race, and that is white heat. With those who disgrace their sacred trust of motherhood we have nothing in common. Our ears are not deaf to the cry that is ever ascending from the battlefield from men of flesh and blood whose indomitable courage is borne to us, so to speak, on every blast of the wind. We women pass on the human ammunition of "only sons" to fill up the gaps, so that when the "common soldier" looks back before going "over the top" he may see the women of the British race on his heels, reliable, dependent, uncomplaining.

The reinforcements of women are, therefore, behind the "common soldier." We gentle-nurtured, timid sex did not want the war. It is no pleasure to us to have our homes made desolate and the apple of our eye taken away. We would sooner our lovable, promising, rollicking boy stayed at school. We would have much preferred to have gone on in a light-hearted way with our amusements and our hobbies. But the bugle call came, and we have hung up the tennis racquet, we've fetched our laddie from school, we've put his cap away, and we have glanced lovingly over his last report, which said "Excellent"—we've wrapped them all in a Union Jack and locked them up, to be taken out only after the war to be looked at. A "common soldier," perhaps, did not count on the women, but they have their part to play, and we have risen to our responsibility. We are proud of our men, and they in turn have to be proud of us. If the men fail, Tommy Atkins, the women won't.

> Tommy Atkins to the front,
> He has gone to bear the brunt.
> Shall "stay-at-homes" do naught but snivel and but sigh?
>
> No, while your eyes are filling
> We are up and doing, willing
> To face the music with you—or to die!

Women are created for the purpose of giving life, and men to take it. Now we are giving it in a double sense. It's not likely we are going to fail Tommy. We shall not flinch one iota, but when the war is over he must not grudge us, when we hear the bugle call of "lights out," a brief, very brief, space of time to withdraw into our own secret chambers and share with Rachel the Silent the lonely anguish of a bereft heart, and to look once more on the college cap, before we emerge stronger women to carry on the glorious work our men's memories have handed down to us for now and all eternity.—Yours, &c., A LITTLE MOTHER.

August 14.

[Owing to the immense demand from home and from the trenches for this letter, which appeared in *The Morning Post*, the Editor found it necessary to place it in the hands of London publishers to be reprinted in pamphlet form, seventy-five thousand copies of which were sold in less than a week direct from the publishers.]

Sergeant-Major Money

It wasn't our battalion, but we lay alongside it,
    So the story is as true as the telling is frank.
They hadn't one Line-officer left, after Arras,
    Except a batty major and the Colonel, who drank.

"B" Company Commander was fresh from the Depot,
    An expert on gas drill, otherwise a dud;
So Sergeant-Major Money carried on, as instructed,
    And that's where the swaddies began to sweat blood.

His Old Army humour was so well-spiced and hearty
    That one poor sod shot himself, and one lost his wits;
But discipline's maintained, and back in rest-billets
    The Colonel congratulates "B" company on their kits.

The subalterns went easy, as was only natural
    With a terror like Money driving the machine,
Till finally two Welshmen, butties from the Rhondda,
    Bayoneted their bugbear in a field-canteen.

Well, we couldn't blame the officers, they relied on Money;
    We couldn't blame the pitboys, their courage was grand;
Or, at least of all, blame Money, an old stiff surviving
    In a New (bloody) Army he couldn't understand.

Robert Graves

One leaf that had gone pretty yellow by now was the hope of perfect victory—swift, unsoured, unruinous, knightly: St. George's over the dragon, David's over Goliath. Some people at home seem to be still clinging hard to that first pretty vision of us as a gifted, lithe, wise little Jack fighting down an unwieldy, dastardly giant. But troops in the field become realists. Ours had seen their side visibly swelling for more than two years, till Jack had become a heavier weight than the giant and yet could not finish him off. We knew that our allies and we outnumbered the Germans and theirs. We knew we were just as well armed. We had seen Germans advancing under our fire and made no mistake about what they were worth. Our first vision of victory had gone the way of its frail sister dream of a perfect Allied comradeship. French soldiers sneered at British now, and British at French. Both had the same derisive note in the voice when they named the "Brav' Belges". Canadians and Australians had almost ceased to take the pains to break it to us gently that they were the "storm troops", the men who had to be sent for to do the tough jobs; that, out of all us sorry home troops, only the Guards Division, two kilted divisions and three English ones could be said to know how to fight. "The English let us down again"; "The Tommies gave us a bad flank, as usual"—these were the stirring things you would hear if you called upon an Australian division a few hours after a battle in which the lion had fought by the side of his whelps. Chilly, autumnal things; while you listened, the war was apparelled no longer in the celestial light of its spring.

from *Disenchantment* by C. E. Montague

FOR SALE.
THE SALIENT ESTATE.
COMPLETE IN EVERY DETAIL.

INTENDING PURCHASERS WILL BE SHOWN ROUND ANYTIME DAY OR NIGHT
UNDERGROUND RESIDENCES READY FOR HABITATION.

—o—o—o—o—

Splendid Motoring Estate! Shooting Perfect!! Fishing Good!!!

—o—o—o—o—

NOW'S THE TIME.   HAVE A STAKE IN THE COUNTRY.
NO REASONABLE OFFER REFUSED.
DO FOR HOME FOR INEBRIATES OR OTHER CHARITABLE INSTITUTION.

Delay is dangerous!   You might miss it!!

—o—o—o—o—

Apply for particulars, etc., to

Thomas, Atkins, Sapper & Co., Zillebeke and Hooge.

HOUSEBREAKERS: WOOLEY, BEAR, CRUMP & CO.   TELEGRAMS: "ADSUM, WIPERS."

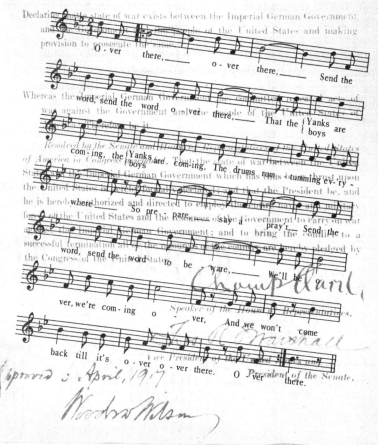

... No pen or drawing can convey this country—the normal setting of the battles taking place day and night, month after month. Evil and the incarnate fiend alone can be master of this war, and no glimmer of God's hand is seen anywhere. Sunset and sunrise are blasphemous, they are mockeries to man, only the black rain out of the bruised and swollen clouds all through the bitter black of night is fit atmosphere in such a land. The rain drives on, the stinking mud becomes more evilly yellow, the shell holes fill up with green-white water, the roads and tracks are covered in inches of slime, the black dying trees ooze and sweat and the shells never cease. They alone plunge overhead, tearing away the rotting tree stumps, breaking the plank roads, striking down horses and mules, annihilating, maiming, maddening, they plunge into the grave which is this land; one huge grave, and cast up on it the poor dead. It is unspeakable, godless, hopeless. I am no longer an artist interested and curious, I am a messenger who will bring back word from the men who are fighting to those who want the war to go on for ever. Feeble, inarticulate, will be my message, but it will have a bitter truth, and may it burn their lousy souls.

from Outline by Paul Nash

Memorial Tablet
(Great War)

Squire nagged and bullied till I went to fight,
(Under Lord Derby's Scheme). I died in hell—
(They called it Passchendaele). My wound was slight,
And I was hobbling back; and then a shell
Burst slick upon the duck-boards: so I fell
Into the bottomless mud, and lost the light.

At sermon-time, while Squire is in his pew,
He gives my gilded name a thoughtful stare;
For, though low down upon the list, I'm there;
"*In proud and glorious memory*" . . . that's my due.
Two bleeding years I fought in France, for Squire:
I suffered anguish that he's never guessed.
Once I came home on leave: and then went west . . .
What greater glory could a man desire?

Siegfried Sassoon

SPECIAL ORDER OF THE DAY
By FIELD-MARSHAL SIR DOUGLAS HAIG
K.T., G.C.B., G.C.V.O., K.C.I.E
Commander-in-Chief, British Armies in France.

D. Haig. F.M.

To ALL RANKS OF THE BRITISH ARMY IN FRANCE AND FLANDERS.

Three weeks ago to-day the enemy began his terrific attacks against us on a fifty-mile front. His objects are to separate us from the French, to take the Channel Ports and destroy the British Army.

In spite of throwing already 106 Divisions into the battle and enduring the most reckless sacrifice of human life, he has as yet made little progress towards his goals.

We owe this to the determined fighting and self-sacrifice of our troops. Words fail me to express the admiration which I feel for the splendid resistance offered by all ranks of our Army under the most trying circumstances.

Many amongst us now are tired. To those I would say that Victory will belong to the side which holds out the longest. The French Army is moving rapidly and in great force to our support.

There is no other course open to us but to fight it out. Every position must be held to the last man: there must be no retirement. With our backs to the wall and believing in the justice of our cause each one of us must fight on to the end. The safety of our homes and the Freedom of mankind alike depend upon the conduct of each one of us at this critical moment.

D. Haig. F.M.

General Headquarters,
Thursday, April 11th, 1918.

Commander-in-Chief,
British Armies in France.

I Know Where to Find 'Em

If you want the old batt-al-ion, We know where they are, we know where they are, We know where they are, If you want the old batt-al-ion, We know where they are, They're hang-ing on the old barbed wire. We've seen 'em, we've seen 'em, Hang-ing on the old barbed wire. We've seen 'em, we've seen 'em, Hang-ing on the old barbed wire.—

L. Barrett

We are lying out in front of our wire, waiting for the signal to leap up. It is quiet. Now and then a white Very light sizzles into the air and illuminates the field as though it were daytime.

We lie perfectly still.

Over in the German lines we hear voices—they are about fifty yards from where we now lie.

I look at the phosphorescent lights on the face of my watch.

Two minutes to go.

MacLeod, the officer in charge of the raiding party, crawls over to where we lie and gives us a last warning.

"Remember," he whispers, "red flares on our parapets is the signal to come back. . . ."

In that instant the sky behind us is stabbed with a thousand flashes of flame.

The earth shakes.

The air hisses, whistles, screams over our heads.

They are firing right into the trenches in front of us.

Clouds of earth leap into the air.

The barrage lasts a minute and then lifts to cut off the enemy's front line from his supports.

In that moment we spring up.

We fire as we run.

The enemy has not had time to get back on his firing-steps. There is no reply to our fire.

We race on.

Fifty yards—forty yards—thirty yards!

My brain is unnaturally cool. I think to myself: This is a raid, you ought to be excited and nervous. But I am calm.

Twenty yards!

I can see the neatly-piled sandbags on the enemy parapets.

Our guns are still thundering behind us.

Suddenly yellow, blinding bursts of flame shoot up from the ground in front of us.

Above the howl of the artillery I hear a man scream as he is hit.

Hand grenades!

We race on.

We fire our rifles from the hip as we run.

The grenades cease to bark.

Ten yards!

With a yell we plunge towards the parapets and jump, bayonets first, into the trench.

Two men are in the bay into which we leap. Half a dozen of our men fall upon them and stab them down into a corner. . . .

I run down the trench looking for prisoners. Each man is for himself.

I am alone.

I turn the corner of a bay. My bayonet points forward—on guard.

I proceed cautiously.

Something moves in the corner of the bay. It is a German. I recognize the pot-shaped helmet.

I lunge forward, aiming at his stomach. It is a lightning, instinctive movement. In that second he twists and reaches for his revolver.

The thrust jerks my body. Something heavy collides with the point of my weapon.

I become insane.

I want to strike again and again. But I cannot. My bayonet does not come clear. I pull, tug, jerk. It does not come out.

I have caught him between his ribs. The bones grip my blade. I cannot withdraw.

Of a sudden I hear him shriek. It sounds far-off as though heard in the moment of waking from a dream.

I have a man at the end of my bayonet, I say to myself.

His shrieks become louder and louder.

We are facing each other—four feet of space separates us.

His eyes are distended; they seem all whites, and look as though they will leap out of their sockets.

There is froth in the corners of his mouth which opens and shuts like that of a fish out of water.

His hands grasp the barrel of my rifle and he joins me in the effort to withdraw. I do not know what to do.

He looks at me piteously.

I put my foot up against his body and try to kick him off. He shrieks into my face.

He will not come off.

I kick him again and again. No use.

His howling unnerves me. I feel I will go insane if I stay in this hole much longer. . . .

It is too much for me. Suddenly I drop the butt of my rifle. He collapses into the corner of the bay. His hands still grip the barrel. I start to run down the bay.

A few steps and I turn the corner.

I am in the next bay. I am glad I cannot see him. I am bewildered.

Out of the roar of the bombardment I think I hear voices. In a flash I remember that I am unarmed. My rifle—it stands between me and death—and it is in the body of him who lies there trying to pull it out.

I am terrified.

If they come here and find me they will stab me just as I stabbed him—and maybe in the ribs, too.

I run back a few paces but I cannot bring myself to turn the corner of the bay in which he lies. I hear his calls for help. The other voices sound nearer.

I am back in the bay.

He is propped up against his parados. The rifle is in such a position that he cannot move. His neck is limp and he rolls his head over his chest until he sees me.

Behind our lines the guns light the sky with monster dull red flashes. In this flickering light this German and I enact our tragedy.

I move to seize the butt of my rifle. Once more we are face to face. He grabs the barrel with a childish movement which seems to say: You may not take it, it is mine. I push his hands away. I pull again.

My tugging and pulling works the blade in his insides.

Again those horrible shrieks!

I place the butt of the rifle under my arm and turn away, trying to drag the blade out. It will not come.

I think. I can get it out if I unfasten the bayonet from the rifle. But I cannot go through with the plan, for the blade is in up to the hilt and the wound which I have been clumsily mauling is now a gaping hole. I cannot put my hand there.

Suddenly I remember what I must do.

I turn around and pull my breech-lock back. The click sounds sharp and clear.

He stops his screaming. He looks at me, silently now.

He knows what I am going to do.

A white Very light soars over our heads. His helmet has fallen from his head. I see his boyish face. He looks like a Saxon; he is fair and under the light I see white down against green cheeks.

I pull my trigger. There is a loud report. The blade at the end of my rifle snaps in two. He falls into the corner of the bay and rolls over. He lies still.

I am free.

from Generals Die in Bed by Charles Yale Harrison

August 8th was the black day of the German Army in the history of this war. . . . Early on August 8th, in a dense fog, rendered still thicker by artificial means, the English, mainly with Australian and Canadian divisions, and the French attacked between Albert and Moreuil with strong squadrons of tanks, but otherwise in no great superiority. Between the Somme and the Luce they penetrated deep into our positions. The divisions in line at that point allowed themselves to be completely overwhelmed. . . .

By the early hours of the forenoon of August 8th I had already gained a complete impression of the situation. It was a very gloomy one. I immediately dispatched a General Staff officer to the battlefield, in order to obtain an idea of the condition of the troops. . . .

Our reserves dwindled. The losses of the enemy, on the other hand, had been extraordinarily small. The balance of numbers had moved heavily against us; it was bound to become increasingly unfavourable as more American troops came in. There was no hope of materially improving our position by a counter-attack. Our only course, therefore, was to hold on.

We had to resign ourselves now to the prospect of a continuation of the enemy's offensive. Their success had been too easily gained. Their wireless was jubilant, and announced—and with truth—that the morale of the German Army was no longer what it had been. The enemy had also captured many documents of inestimable value to them. . . .

The report of the Staff officer I had sent to the battlefield as to the condition of those divisions which had met the first shock of the attack on the 8th perturbed me deeply. I summoned divisional commanders and officers from the line to Avesnes to discuss events with them in detail. I was told of deeds of glorious valour, but of behaviour which, I openly confess, I should not have thought possible in the German Army; whole bodies of our men had surrendered to single troopers, or isolated squadrons.

Retiring troops, meeting a fresh division going bravely into action, had shouted out things like "Blackleg", and "You're prolonging the war", expressions that were to be heard again later. The officers in many places had lost their influence and allowed themselves to be swept along with the rest. . . . A battalion commander from the front, who came out with a draft from home shortly before August 8th, attributed this to the spirit of insubordination and the atmosphere which the men brought back with them from home. Everything I had feared, and of which I had so often given warning, had here, in one place, become a reality. Our war machine was no longer efficient. Our fighting power had suffered, even though the great majority of divisions still fought heroically.

The 8th of August put the decline of that fighting power beyond all doubt, and in such a situation as regards reserves I had no hope of finding a strategic expedient whereby to turn the situation to our advantage. On the contrary, I became convinced that we were now without that safe foundation for the plans of G.H.Q. on which I had hitherto been able to build, at least so far as this is possible in war. Leadership now assumed, as I then stated, the character of an irresponsible game of chance, a thing I have always considered fatal.

The fate of the German people was for me too high a stake. The war must be ended.

from My War Memories, 1914–18 by General Ludendorff

Anthem for Doomed Youth

What passing-bells for these who die as cattle?
  Only the monstrous anger of the guns.
  Only the stuttering rifles' rapid rattle
Can patter out their hasty orisons.
No mockeries for them from prayers or bells,
  Nor any voice of mourning save the choirs,—
The shrill, demented choirs of wailing shells;
  And bugles calling for them from sad shires.

What candles may be held to speed them all?
  Not in the hands of boys, but in their eyes
Shall shine the holy glimmers of goodbyes.
  The pallor of girls' brows shall be their pall;
Their flowers the tenderness of silent minds,
And each slow dusk a drawing-down of blinds.

Wilfred Owen

Waking, Paradis and I look at each other, and remember. We return to life and daylight as in a nightmare. In front of us the calamitous plain is resurrected, where hummocks vaguely appear from their immersion, the steel-like plain that is rusty in places and shines with lines and pools of water, while bodies are strewn here and there in the vastness like foul rubbish, prone bodies that breathe or rot.

Paradis says to me, "That's war."

"Yes, that's it," he repeats in a far-away voice, "that's war. It's not anything else."

He means—and I am with him in his meaning—"More than attacks that are like ceremonial reviews, more than visible battles unfurled like banners, more even than the hand-to-hand encounters of shouting strife, War is frightful and unnatural weariness, water up to the belly, mud and dung and infamous filth. It is befouled faces and tattered flesh, it is the corpses that are no longer like corpses even, floating on the ravenous earth. It is that, that endless monotony of misery, broken by poignant tragedies; it is that, and not the bayonet's silvery glitter, nor the trumpet's cock-crow in the sun!

Paradis, possessed by his notion, waved his hand towards the wide unspeakable landscape, and looking steadily on it repeated his sentence, "War is *that*. It is that everywhere. What are we, we chaps, and what's all this here? Nothing at all. All we can see is only a speck. You've got to remember that this morning there's three thousand kilometres of equal evils, or nearly equal, or worse."

"And then," said the comrade at our side, whom we could not recognize even by his voice, "tomorrow it begins again. It began again the day before yesterday, and all the days before that!"

With an effort as if he was tearing the ground, the chasseur dragged his body out of the earth where he had moulded a depression like an oozing coffin, and sat in the hole. He blinked his eyes and tried to shake the valance of mud from his face, and said, "We shall come out of it again this time. And who knows, p'raps we shall come out of it again tomorrow! Who knows?"

Paradis, with his back bent under mats of earth and clay, was trying to convey his idea that the war cannot be imagined or measured in terms of time and space. "When one speaks of the whole war," he said, thinking aloud, "it's as if you said nothing at all—the words are strangled. We're here, and we look at it all like blind men."

A bass voice rolled to us from a little farther away, "No, one cannot imagine it."

At these words a burst of harsh laughter tore itself from some one. "How could you imagine it, to begin with, if you hadn't been there?"

"You'd have to be mad," said the chasseur.

Paradis leaned over a sprawling outspread mass beside him and said, "Are you asleep?"

"No, but I'm not going to budge." The smothered and terror-struck mutter issued instantly from the mass that was covered with a thick and slimy horse-cloth, so indented that it seemed to have been trampled. "I'll tell you why. I believe my belly's shot through. But I'm not sure, and I daren't find out."

"Let's see—"

"No, not yet," says the man. "I'd rather stop on a bit like this."

The others, dragging themselves on their elbows, began to make splashing movements, by way of casting off the clammy infernal covering that weighed them down. The paralysis of cold was passing away from the knot of sufferers, though the light no longer made any progress over the great irregular marsh of the lower plain. The desolation proceeded, but not the day.

Then he who spoke sorrowfully, like a bell, said, "It'll be no good telling about it, eh? They wouldn't believe you; not out of malice or through liking to pull your leg, but because they couldn't. When you say to 'em later, if you live to say it, 'We were on a night job and we got shelled and we were very nearly drowned in mud,' they'll say, 'Ah!' And p'raps they'll say, 'You didn't have a very spicy time on the job.' And that's all. No one can know it. Only us."

"No, not even us, not even us!" some one cried.

"That's what I say, too. We shall forget—we're forgetting already, my boy!"

"We've seen too much to remember."

"And everything we've seen was too much. We're not *made* to hold it all. It takes its bloody hook in all directions. We're too little to hold it."

"You're right, we *shall* forget! Not only the length of the big misery, which can't be reckoned, as you say, ever since the beginning, but the marches that turn up the ground and turn it again, lacerating your feet and wearing out your bones under a load that seems to grow bigger in the sky, the exhaustion until you don't know your own name any more, the tramping and the inaction that grind you, the digging jobs that exceed your strength, the endless vigils when you fight against sleep and watch for an enemy who is everywhere in the night, the pillows of dung and lice—we shall forget not only those, but even the foul wounds of shells and machine-guns, the mines, the gas, and the counter-attacks. At those moments you're full of the excitement of reality, and you've some satisfaction. But all that wears off and goes away, you don't know how and you don't know where, and there's only the names left, only the words of it, like in a dispatch."

"That's true what he says," remarks a man, without moving his head in its pillory of mud. "When I was on leave, I found I'd already jolly well forgotten what had happened to me before. There were some letters from me that I read over again just as if they were a book I was opening. And yet in spite of that, I've forgotten also all the pain I've had in the war. We're forgetting-machines. Men are things that think a little but chiefly forget. That's what we are."

"Then neither the other side nor us'll remember! So much misery all wasted!"

This thought increased the abasement of these beings on the shore of the flood, like news of a great disaster, and humiliated them still more.

"Ah, if one *did* remember!" cried some one.

"If we remembered," said another, "there wouldn't be any more war."

A third added grandly, "Yes, if we remembered, war would be less useless than it is."

But suddenly one of the prone survivors rose to his knees, dark as a great bat ensnared, and as the mud dripped from his waving arms he cried in a hollow voice, "There must be no more war after this!"

In that miry corner where, still feeble unto impotence, we were beset by blasts of wind which laid hold on us with such rude strength that the very ground seemed to sway like sea-drift, the cry of the man who looked as if he were trying to fly away evoked other like cries: "There must be no more war after this!"

The sullen or furious exclamations of these men fettered to the earth, incarnate of earth, arose and slid away on the wind like beating wings—

"No more war! No more war! Enough of it!"

"It's too stupid—it's too stupid," they mumbled. "What does it mean, at the bottom of it, all this?—all this that you can't even give a name to?"

They snarled and growled like wild beasts on that sort of ice-floe contended for by the elements, in their dismal disguise of ragged mud. So huge was the protest thus rousing them in revolt that it choked them.

"We're made to live, not to be done in like this!"

"Men are made to be husbands, fathers—*men*, what the devil!—

not beasts that hunt each other and cut each other's throats and make themselves stink like all that."

"And yet, everywhere—everywhere—there are beasts, savage beasts or smashed beasts. Look, look!"

I shall never forget the look of those limitless lands wherefrom the water had corroded all colour and form, whose contours crumbled on all sides under the assault of the liquid putrescence that flowed across the broken bones of stakes and wire and framing; nor, rising above those things amid the sullen Stygian immensity, can I ever forget the vision of the thrill of reason, logic and simplicity that suddenly shook these men like a fit of madness.

I could see them agitated by this idea—that to try to live one's life on earth and to be happy is not only a right but a duty, and even an ideal and a virtue; that the only end of social life is to make easy the inner life of every one.

"To live!"—"All of us!"—"You!"—"Me!"

"No more war—ah, no!—it's too stupid—worse than that, it's too—"

For a finishing echo to their half-formed thought a saying came to the mangled and miscarried murmur of the mob from a filth-crowned face that I saw arise from the level of the earth—

"Two armies fighting each other—that's like one great army committing suicide!"

from *Under Fire* by Henri Barbusse

A Lament

We who are left, how shall we look again
Happily on the sun or feel the rain,
Without remembering how they who went
Ungrudgingly and spent
Their all for us loved, too, the sun and rain?

A bird among the rain-wet lilac sings—
But we, how shall we turn to little things
And listen to the birds and winds and streams
Made holy by their dreams,
Nor feel the heart-break in the heart of things?

Wilfrid Wilson Gibson

POSTSCRIPT

Apologia Pro Poemate Meo

I, too, saw God through mud,—
    The mud that cracked on cheeks when wretches smiled.
    War brought more glory to their eyes than blood,
    And gave their laughs more glee than shakes a child.

Merry it was to laugh there—
    Where death becomes absurd and life absurder.
    For power was on us as we slashed bones bare
    Not to feel sickness or remorse of murder.

I, too, have dropped off fear—
    Behind the barrage, dead as my platoon,
    And sailed my spirit surging light and clear
    Past the entanglement where hopes lay strewn;

And witnessed exultation—
    Faces that used to curse me, scowl for scowl,
    Shine and lift up with passion of oblation,
    Seraphic for an hour; though they were foul.

I have made fellowships—
    Untold of happy lovers in old song.
    For love is not the binding of fair lips
    With the soft silk of eyes that look and long,

By Joy, whose ribbon slips,—
    But wound with war's hard wire whose stakes are strong;
    Bound with the bandage of the arm that drips;
    Knit in the webbing of the rifle-thong.

I have perceived much beauty
    In the hoarse oaths that kept our courage straight;
    Heard music in the silentness of duty;
    Found peace where shell-storms spouted reddest spate.

Nevertheless, except you share
    With them in hell the sorrowful dark of hell,
    Whose world is but the trembling of a flare,
    And heaven but as the highway for a shell,

You shall not hear their mirth:
    You shall not come to think them well content
    By any jest of mine. These men are worth
    Your tears. You are not worth their merriment.

Wilfred Owen

FURTHER SOURCE MATERIAL

Autobiography and Personal Accounts

EDMUND BLUNDEN   *Undertones of War*   Collins
SIR PHILIP GIBBS   *The War Dispatches*   Tandem
ROBERT GRAVES   *Goodbye to All That*   Cassell (*also* Penguin)
T. E. LAWRENCE   *Seven Pillars of Wisdom*   Cape (*also* Penguin)
CECIL LEWIS   *Sagittarius Rising*   Peter Davies (*also* Corgi)
WYNDHAM LEWIS   *Blasting and Bombardiering*   Calder
SIR COMPTON MACKENZIE   *Gallipoli Memories*   Cassell
C. E. MONTAGUE   *Disenchantment*   MacGibbon & Kee
SIR HERBERT READ   *Annals of Innocence and Experience*   Faber
SIEGFRIED SASSOON   *Memoirs of a Fox-hunting Man*   Faber
      Memoirs of an Infantry Officer   Faber
      Sherston's Progress   Faber
      Siegfried's Journey   Faber

Fiction Based on Personal Experience

HENRI BARBUSSE   *Under Fire*   Dent
IAN HAY (JOHN HAY BEITH)   *The First Hundred Thousand*   Leo Cooper
ERNEST HEMINGWAY   *A Farewell to Arms*   Cape (*also* Penguin)
FREDERIC MANNING   *Her Privates We*   Peter Davies
ERNEST RAYMOND   *Tell England*   Cassell
ERICH MARIA REMARQUE   *All Quiet on the Western Front*   Putnam
                  (*also* Mayflower)
HENRY WILLIAMSON   *How Dear Is Life*   Macdonald
      A Fox Under My Cloak   Macdonald
      The Golden Virgin   Macdonald
      Love and the Loveless   Macdonald
      A Test to Destruction   Macdonald

Histories

JOHN BROPHY and ERIC PARTRIDGE   *The Long Trail*   Deutsch
                  (*also* Sphere)
L. F. HOBLEY   *The First World War*   Blackie
ARTHUR MARWICK   *The Deluge*   Bodley Head (*also* Penguin)
A. J. P. TAYLOR   *The First World War*   Penguin
Purnell's *History of the First World War*

Poetry

BRIAN GARDNER *Up the Line to Death* Methuen
DAVID JONES *In Parenthesis* Faber
WILFRED OWEN *Collected Poems* Chatto & Windus
I. M. PARSONS *Men Who March Away* Chatto & Windus
SIEGFRIED SASSOON *Collected Poems* Faber

Records

BBC *Scrapbook for 1914* Fontana
What Passing Bell Argo

INDEX

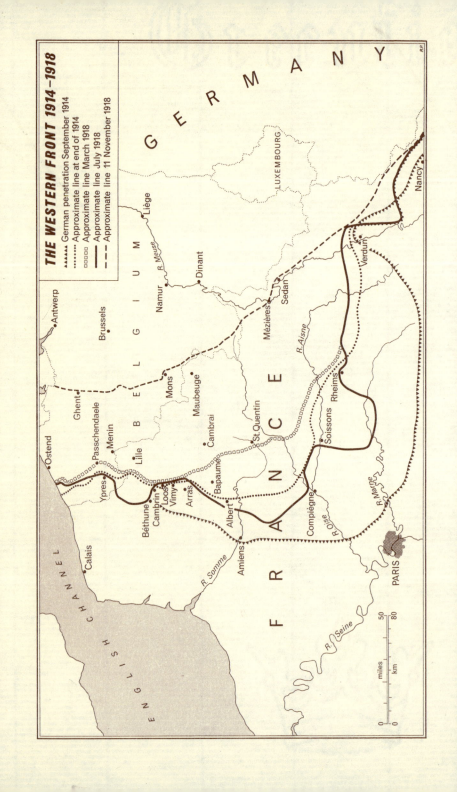

THE WESTERN FRONT 1914–1918

▲▲▲▲▲ German penetration September 1914
∙∙∙∙∙∙ Approximate line at end of 1914
▫▫▫▫▫ Approximate line March 1918
▬▬▬ Approximate line July 1918
▬ ▬ ▬ Approximate line 11 November 1918

GERMANY

LUXEMBOURG

BELGIUM

FRANCE

ENGLISH CHANNEL

Antwerp

Brussels

Liège

Namur

R. Meuse

Dinant

Ghent

Mons

Maubeuge

Cambrai

St. Quentin

Mézières

Sedan

R. Aisne

Rheims

Soissons

Verdun

Nancy

Ostend

Passchendaele

Menin

Lille

Ypres

Béthune

Cambrin

Loos

Vimy

Arras

Bapaume

Albert

Compiègne

R. Oise

R. Marne

Calais

R. Somme

Amiens

PARIS

R. Seine

miles
km
0   50
0   80